Writers and Politics
in Modern Germany
(1918–1945)

C. E. Williams

HODDER AND STOUGHTON
LONDON SYDNEY AUCKLAND TORONTO

Writers and Politics in Modern Germany is one of a series of books under the general editorship of Professor John Flower. The other books in the series are as follows:

Writers and Politics in Modern Britain (J. A. Morris)
Writers and Politics in Modern France (J. E. Flower)
Writers and Politics in Modern Italy (J. A. Gatt-Rutter)
Writers and Politics in Modern Scandinavia (Janet Mawby)
Writers and Politics in Modern Spain (J. Butt)
Writers and Politics in Modern Russia (M. A. Nicholson)

ISBN 0 340 18442 6
First published 1977
Printed in Great Britain for Hodder and Stoughton Educational,
a division of Hodder and Stoughton Ltd,
Mill Road, Dunton Green, Sevenoaks, Kent,
by Richard Clay (The Chaucer Press), Ltd,
Bungay, Suffolk.

Foreword

The term 'political literature' like 'committed literature' with which it is frequently associated has become an accepted part of the language of literary history. Yet however convenient, it is, on examination, surprisingly imprecise and misleading. The whole area of the interaction between politics and literature is a vast and complex one which has yet, especially on a European scale, to be fully and comprehensively charted. Certainly invaluable contributions do already exist: Jean-Paul Sartre's *Qu'est-ce que la littérature?* (1947), George Woodcock's *The Writer and Politics* (1948), Jürgen Rühle's *Literatur und Revolution* (1960), Irving Howe's *Politics and the Novel* (1961), John Mander's *The Writer and Commitment* (1961) for example. There are, too, as the bibliographical information contained in the individual essays in this series will reveal, a number of equally important books which deal with the issue in purely national terms. With few exceptions, however, these, like many of the more general studies, suffer from the same defects resulting in the main from a failure to distinguish adequately between 'political literature' and what might be termed 'social literature', and from an incomplete assessment of changes both in political climates and in the writer's relationship to society as a whole. Yet, even when the area of investigation and terminology has been more carefully ascertained, we often find that these books are principally concerned either with an examination of the political ideas *per se* contained in various works of literature, or with an assessment of the ways in which parties and movements have controlled and used to best advantage writers and intellectuals who claim political allegiance. More recently Roland Barthes in *Le Degré Zéro de l'écriture* (1967), George Steiner in *Language and Silence* (1967) and David Caute in *Illusion* (1971) have suggested a wider perspective, outlining some of the problems of style and form which an imaginative writer has to face when he offers his pen to a political (or social) cause. On the whole, however, it is fair to say that the majority of critics have concentrated more on *what* ideas are expressed than on *how* they have been. In addition therefore to attempting to define the concept of political literature more precisely and to exploring such issues as the suitability of imaginative literature as a vehicle for political ideas or the effect such literature can have on the public for example, one of the principal concerns of these essays is to attempt to examine ways in which an author's political sympathy or affiliation can be seen to affect or even dictate the way in which he writes. In some countries—in Russia, France or Spain, for example—direct influence of this kind is more apparent than in others. Elsewhere, notably in Britain, where political directives concerning art and literature have not been the rule, the problem is in some ways more difficult to assess. Indeed national variation of this kind is one of the principal contributory factors to the complex nature of the whole question. Thus while the subject is best illustrated and examined in the literature of France and Germany during the interwar years, it is after the Second World War that it fully emerges in the works of Italian and Scandinavian writers. Furthermore literary experiment seen and approved in some countries as an expression of a progressive, even revolutionary, political position is considered in others to be characteristic of subversion and decadence.

Given such problems as these and given too the amount of space available, these seven small volumes can do little more than hope to encourage a new approach to political literature. While free to explore the subject in the way they believe to be most useful within the context of the literary history of their particular countries, contributors have been encouraged to balance general comment with examination of specific examples. Inevitably therefore the essays appear arbitrarily selective. But like the literature which they choose to examine it is hoped that they will be judged not only for what they contain but also for the ways in which they deal with it.

John Flower

General Bibliography

The following are a selection of those books which discuss some of the general problems associated with this subject. Suggestions for further reading are contained in the notes to individual essays.

BARTHES, Roland, *Le Degré Zéro de l'écriture*, Editions du Seuil, Paris, 1953 (Translated: *Writing Degree Zero*, Cape, London, 1967).

CAUTE, David, *Illusion: An Essay on Politics, Theatre and the Novel*, Deutsch, London, 1971.

CROSSMAN, Richard, *The God that Failed: Six Studies in Communism*, Hamish Hamilton, London, 1950.

HOWE, Irving, *Politics and the Novel*, Horizon Press, New York, 1955.

MANDER, John, *The Writer and Commitment*, Secker & Warburg, London, 1961.

MUIR, Edwin, *Essays on Literature and Society*, Hogarth Press, London, 1965.

PANICHAS, George A. (ed.), *The Politics of Twentieth-Century Novelists*, Crowell, New York, 1974.

RÜHLE ,Jürgen, *Literatur und Revolution*, Kiepenheuer & Witsch, 1960 (Translated: *Literature and Revolution*, Pall Mall, London, 1969).

SARTRE, Jean-Paul, *Qu'est-ce que la littérature?* Gallimard, Paris, 1948 (Translated: *What is Literature?* Methuen, London, 1951).

STEINER, George, *Language and Silence: Essays and Notes, 1958–66*, Faber, London, 1967.

TROTSKY, Leon, *Literature and Revolution*, University of Michigan Press, Ann Arbor, 1960.

WINEGARTEN, Renee, *Writers and Revolution: the fatal lure of action*, Franklin Watts, New York, 1974.

WOODCOCK, George, *The Writer and Politics*, The Porcupine Press, London, 1948.

Contents

'. . . a human situation is characterizable only when one has also taken into account those conceptions which the participants have of it, how they experience their tensions in this situation and how they react to the tensions so conceived.'

Karl Mannheim

Preface

The history of political literature in Germany has yet to be written. What follows is a contribution to the story of literary commitment in our century. But I have restricted the scope of my enquiry still further, to the years 1918 to 1945. This decision was only in part dictated by lack of space. It is my belief that the development of political writing in Germany since the Second World War has not fundamentally altered the issues in debate or the lines along which the aesthetic battle has been fought. Of course certain techniques have been refined. But others such as socialist realism or *Heimatdichtung* stubbornly survive in their respective halves of Germany. Something akin to the 'internal emigration' of the Nazi era has emerged in the lyrical poetry and allegorical prose of the GDR, while in the Federal Republic the debate about 'proletarian literature' has progressed little since the last years of Weimar, except that the tables have been turned on the Zhdanovites and the disciples of Tolstoy. If overt fascists no longer enjoy a hearing among the intellectuals, the argument between conservatism and radicalism, between *l'art pour l'art* and commitment, continues unabated, with all the sterility of reiterated ideological prejudices. And the homeless centre-left still finds itself in no-man's land, a third force of perpetual opposition, preserving its integrity but apparently condemned to impotence or to being modishly patronized.

Yet some things clearly have changed, above all the writer's relationship with his public. In the Weimar period intellectuals on all sides enjoyed a rare *rapport* with their audience and a firm sense of their own 'representative' position, of their allegiance to a particular social group or class whose values and interests they were pledged to articulate. The growing awareness that a decisive ideological and political battle was impending helped to simplify the issues and to justify commitment. The prestige of the intelligentsia inspired them with confidence in their ability to have a direct and immediate impact upon the course of events. Since then Hitler, Stalin and the development of Western society have between them reduced this confidence to a mere shadow of its former self. The issues have grown labyrinthine in their complexity. Ambiguity and irony seem more reliable lode-stars than faith. Pessimism is our birthright. We can no longer delude ourselves into believing that ideology can cure our ills. In many respects the post-war debate about commitment in literature came to an end with the Cold War. The political function of the writer is now seen as something far more modest and more fundamental than was once the case—the liberating of language itself from corruption and manipulation, not for the sake of aesthetic purity, but in the interests of social man. Thus I return to my starting point: the Weimar Republic and the Third Reich offer a paradigm of German political writing in our century, intensified, concentrated, exaggerated even, but exemplary in its range of possibilities. Where the nature of post-war commitment diverges from it, we find a systematic narrowing-down rather than an amplification of its erstwhile hopes and methods.

Within the period 1918–45 I have again had to be selective for purely practical reasons. In an attempt to combine a sense of context and perspective with the particular detail of the individual work, I have provided in each section a general impression of the literature associated with my various themes, followed by a closer look at representative examples. The choice of examples is based on their significance in the intellectual or political climate of their time, as attested by debate or controversy; or on their sales figures, a criterion which may be debatable as an indication of literary value but at least suggests a documentary interest and a potential political importance. Occasionally I have relied on my own subjective judgement in selecting works to complement the alternatives suggested by the first two criteria. I have kept biographical information down to a minimum and have dealt very selectively with Bertolt Brecht and Thomas Mann whose careers and achievements are familiar far beyond the purview of German literary historians. Moreover I have deliberately omitted Austrian writers from the present study, since I have already dealt with them in an earlier book, *The Broken Eagle* (London, 1974). There the reader will find discussions of Hugo von Hofmannsthal, Karl Kraus and Joseph Roth, among others, which are also relevant to the current theme.

A major part of my task I saw as the attempt to piece together a coherent pattern of development, and to make available the conclusions of more detailed studies of particular authors and situations. There is thus a strong synoptic bias in my account. I have tried to balance the discussion of theme and subject with a commentary on formal techniques and language, whenever the latter seemed to warrant attention. But since it is in the nature of committed literature to stress content at the expense of aesthetics, the reader will inevitably discover a predominance of interpretation over formal analysis. A 'close reading' of the conventional is a sure recipe for boredom. I have borne in mind the needs of fellow Germanists whose interests have not yet extended to this field of enquiry; and the needs of those students of the subject whose knowledge is based on the literature of other nations. May the former forgive me for often stating the obvious, and the latter for sometimes not being explicit enough. But may they both find here something of interest.

Acknowledgments

In a study as wide-ranging as this it would be invidious to record every single debt. The works listed in the footnotes to my general sections will give some idea of the intellectual sources on which I have drawn. I am also grateful for the often unwitting co-operation of colleagues and students who participated in discussions on these topics. My original interest in the subject dates back to a seminar on twentieth-century German literature given by Professor J. P. Stern at Cambridge in the early sixties. No mere acknowledgment can convey the measure of my indebtedness to him.

Introduction

The Apolitical Tradition

The problematic relationship between spirit and power, right and might is a thread which runs through German intellectual history from the eighteenth century onwards. What has come to be known as the peculiarly 'non-political' quality of the German tradition implies not so much apathy or lack of insight—though these often accompany it—as a fundamental scepticism with regard to the meaning and value of political activity.[1] To be non-political in this sense is to believe that politics has no bearing on the essential areas of human experience, that it is a peripheral affair of concern only to the politicians. This attitude initially produces indifference or contempt towards the political sphere. But under the pressure of events it produces an allied pheno-menon: the justification of political power by reference to spiritual, metaphysical or moral principles—what Alfred Döblin once called 'den Kurzschluss in die Mystik'.[2] A tradition which begins by devaluing political activity ends by participating in it on wholly false assumptions. Instead of seeing politics as the art of acquiring and exercising power, or as an area of practical arrangements in an imperfect world, the non-political mind ignores the mundane criteria of political realism and insists upon transforming the political struggle into a conflict of spiritual principle. From being viewed as the sordid squabbling and manoeuvring of inferior men, politics becomes the arena of world-historical individ-uals, the preserve of the national leader or of a ruling elite. Politics is now seen as a matter of statesmanship and foreign policy, while internal party politicking continues to be treated with contempt. Though the hypostasization of political issues is a familiar feature of other nations at certain points in their history, what is characteristic of Germany is the way in which this process becomes a substitute for the political emancipation of the bourgeoisie.

The non-political tradition was rooted in philosophical Idealism and the social and political conditions of the eighteenth century.[3] The individualism of Kant, Goethe, Humboldt or Schiller had encouraged

7

withdrawal, indifference, contempt and withal acquiescence in the *status quo*. The collectivism of the Romantics, however, produced a witches' brew of mysticism and economics, *Realpolitik* and ethical imperatives, nationalism and spirituality. The individualist strand of Idealism predominated while the class which espoused it was not yet confident enough of its ability to win political power. The collectivist strand predominated when the bourgeoisie grew more conscious of its political importance but chose to ally itself with the old ruling class in the face of pressures from a foreign enemy or from 'the enemy within', the organized working class. Admittedly the period between 1830 and 1848 saw determined attempts to establish another alternative.[4] Liberal and socialist writers applied the methods of rational analysis to their society; they acknowledged the necessary link between the individual and society but argued the case for a critical, dissenting intelligentsia or even ideologically committed literature. The *Jung-Deutschland* Liberals, however, if not Idealists, were still victims of the non-political tradition. In their inexperience and intellectualism, their subjectivism and naïve rationalism, they showed themselves far less interested in social problems than in literary freedom and personal emancipation. Their 'aestheticism' was rejected by the ideological socialists of the 1840s, who renounced creativity in favour of rhetorical didacticism. Heine was the only major imaginative writer who straddled both these literary generations and whose unashamed subjectivism went hand in hand with a perceptive, undogmatic concern for social and political realities. But there was no place for such a voice in Germany either then or later.

The *débâcle* of 1848, when even the Liberals showed themselves attached to class interests and national ambitions, ensured the survival of the authoritarian state. In the years between the abortive revolution and the unification of Germany, many former Liberals escaped into the Idealist tradition; they repudiated *Realpolitik* but allowed Bismarck to pursue it unhindered, provided the state did not interfere with their ability to cultivate the inner life of culture, learning, pure philosophy, the arts and other creations of the spirit.[5] But some intellectuals, like Treitschke, justified Bismarck's policies in spiritual or ethical terms, as the Romantics had glorified feudal absolutism before them, while the National Liberals followed suit on a more mundane level. The crowning success of 1871, the foundation of the German Empire, reinforced these tendencies. The result was not merely an unpalatable idealization of the existing state and its imperial ambitions (following Hegel), but the distraction of educated opinion away from the concrete problems of industrialization and urbanization to hazy notions of the German 'mission' or the vindication of the German 'spirit'. A bourgeoisie dominated by the military and the bureaucracy, uncertain of its own values and deprived of an effective public voice, sought in national aggrandizement a substitute for the rational modernization of its own society.

As Sombart pointed out, the intellectual, confronted by the alternatives of conformism or futile opposition, often turned his back on politics altogether.[6] Wilhelmine Germany can display few commentators with the lucid scepticism and critical irony of the later Fontane, or with the satirical wit of Heinrich Mann. Naturalist descriptions of working-class misery were characterized by a doctrinaire determinism, as contemporary socialist critics were quick to complain. The George circle provided a focal point for the cult of aestheticism and an elitist indifference to politics. When Stefan George proceeded in the early years of the century to formulate an ideal of social hierarchy and charismatic leadership, of heroism and brotherhood, his poetry was remote from concrete realities, yet coincided with the general aura of Wilhelmine authoritarianism.[7] He provides a classic example of the wrong sort of fusion between *Geist* and *Macht*, of power sanctioned by dedication and service to values that derive from a transcendent authority. He was devoted to spiritual and cultural renewal, but by 1914 he was calling for a holy war to purge the sins of liberal materialism and individualism, like the *völkisch* writers before him. In his own rarified idiom George echoed the 'unspoken assumptions' of the age and helped to obscure the real political issues behind a smokescreen of indefinable abstractions.

The wave of national fervour which surged through German society as through much of Europe in August 1914 bore the vast majority of intellectuals along with it. Their impassioned discovery of patriotic feeling stemmed paradoxically from their widespread alienation from politics in the preceding years.[8] Welcomed in from the cold, they rejoined the community of the nation with the fervour of the proselyte. But the war experience, which directly affected so many areas of individual existence hitherto kept apart from the public sphere, served only to increase political awareness without providing the opportunity for political responsibility.[9] Censorship and a form of military dictatorship prevented proper political debate. If the cult of totally detached inwardness became virtually impossible, the nature of political involvement was still governed by the Idealist legacy, now mobilized in an assault on liberal-democratic, 'Western' values. Perhaps the most

9

radical—and certainly the most tortuous—disavowal came from the pen of Thomas Mann in his *Betrachtungen eines Unpolitischen*. Somewhat late in the day Mann tried to reaffirm the individualist cult of inwardness, the need for an inviolate private sphere, within the framework of political authoritarianism.

Under Weimar the tragic consequences of political inexperience became clear; a failure to appreciate the true nature of the difficulties besetting the Republic, and an inability to assess the actual possibilities of the situation or to envisage the political forms that idealism was bound to take in practice. This dangerous lack of insight was compounded by an equally perilous moral intransigence which scorned the compromises and manoeuvring of workaday politics and attempted to realize its dreams and visions in all their pristine strength and purity. This intransigence, as Max Weber foresaw during the winter of the Revolution, and as Heine had prophesied many decades earlier, could all too easily topple over into chiliastic zeal which brooked no obstacle or delay.[10]

There can rarely have been an era so productive of political writing and ideological conflict, or so receptive to committed literature as the Weimar years. But the period also demonstrates the limitations of literary commitment. A generation of German writers which plunged into the political arena as no other had done before it, came to realize how helpless they were to control or influence events through their art. The lesson of Weimar and the Third Reich was not only the need for an intellectual attitude that encompassed socio-political issues in a critical fashion, not only the acknowledgement that the claims of commitment and aesthetic freedom are not easily reconciled: it was also the realization that political literature could at best hope only for oblique and indirect results. The ultimate measure of political writing lay less in the extent to which it inspired political action than in the extent to which it shaped human consciousness. That insight, however, implying as it did that *all* literature has a latent political function, sounded the knell of a tradition which for so long had thrived on a particularly insidious form of false consciousness.

Chapter One
The Literature of War

In the first post-war decade, books about the War were neither numerous nor—with one or two notable exceptions—widely read. It was not until after the publication of Remarque's *Im Westen nichts Neues* in 1928 that a spate of war novels, diaries and memoirs poured on to the market. The majority were influenced by the increasingly violent political conflicts of the final years of the Republic and played a role in preparing the public emotionally and intellectually for the appeal of fascism.[1] Books such as Franz Schauwecker's *Aufbruch der Nation*, Werner Beumelburg's *Sperrfeuer um Deutschland* or his *Gruppe Bosemüller*, Hans Zöberlein's *Der Glaube an Deutschland*, Josef Magnus Wehner's *Sieben vor Verdun* and fresh editions of Walter Flex's wartime work *Der Wanderer zwischen beiden Welten* all helped to shape an image of the war experience which had its parallel and extension in the right-wing ideologies of the Weimar period. Though some of these war books were more explicitly political than others, together they created a myth of the *Kriegserlebnis* which estranged a substantial and militant section of the population from the political realities of the Republic. Their point of departure was the banality and lack of authenticity of Wilhelmine Germany, a world of careerism, material greed, irrelevant examinations and deep social divisions. Most of the heroes of these books are sons of well-to-do bourgeois families, educated and idealistic, sickened by the petty cares of the parental world. Through the War they achieve a spiritual liberation, a breakthrough to a more meaningful and mysterious existence. The touchstone of their moral worth is their reaction to the *Materialschlacht*, the battle of attrition. The books avoid reasoned analysis of the causes or consequences of the War; instead they seek to reproduce the experience which the authors have undergone. Thereby, however, they remain in thrall to the experience, completely subject to its emotional impact and incapable of rising above it to view it with critical detachment. At best they transcend it only through nebulous metaphysical speculation. The War often appears as an inevitable decree of Fate. A naïve religiosity informs many of these accounts, absolving the individual from traditional ethical responsibility and transferring the conflict on to a cosmic plane. Yet the Spirit, Law or Idea which the heroes obey cannot be named, nor can the nature of the new world which they anticipate be described. What is fundamentally at stake is the value of self-sacrifice as such, irrespective of the cause in whose name it occurs. When the vague idealistic gloss on that sacrifice became politicized after the War, it took the form of a Messianic nationalism remote from the concrete possibilities of the time. Paradoxically the war writers condemned the ideological abstractions of contemporary politics and felt that their generation could forge a new reality out of the living experience of the War. One of their prominent themes was that of the comradeship of the trenches which afforded the hope of a better society. The 'community' at the front was classless and united. It judged a man not by material possessions or artificial prestige or an accident of birth but by a supreme test of his moral worth. The unique experience of the front line divided it from the civilian world so that it was able to preserve the values of sacrifice and solidarity at a time when the *Volksgemeinschaft* at home was being betrayed by defeatist politicians. And since the Weimar state was a creature of that cowardly treason, the nationalist ex-servicemen pitted themselves determinedly against what they felt to be its gross utilitarianism, its anarchic party divisions, its moral flabbiness or decadence, and its cult of self-interest. There was a conviction that the war generation had shed its blood for the sake of a new future—the regeneration of the *Volk* which was increasingly identified with the rebirth of a strong, united German state. Such was the context in which the nationalist war writers selected and interpreted their material. They wrote not merely to record or to exorcize their experiences but as part of an ideological campaign. After 1933, even if particular authors fell out of favour with the National Socialist regime, their war books often retained the seal of Party approval because it was felt that they stiffened the moral fibre of the nation. (Ernst Jünger's *In Stahlgewittern* was a case in point.) An older book, Edgar Spiegel's *Kriegstagebuch U202* (1916), was reissued during the Third Reich to become a best-seller, while politically acceptable writers such as Ettighofer produced new war books which found an avid market. Together with the novel of peasant life the literature of war was the most frequently mined seam in the literary life of the Third Reich.

1. Ernst Jünger: *In Stahlgewittern* (1920); *Der Kampf als inneres Erlebnis* (1922)

Jünger was one of the earliest and most influential of the German war writers. He speaks not for a generation but for an elite, a select few who were able to face up to the horror of war and seek in it a validation of their existence quite independent of the political goals for which the War was fought. The value of a cause or an idea is measured in Nietzschean terms by the intensity with which its champions defend it, not by any objective criteria, thus rendering on the political level the theme of the 'dear purchase' which one critic deems to be a dominant motif of the greatest literary achievements and the ruling ideology of the age: a salvation whose value is relative to the degree of difficulty, arduousness and hardness that attends it.[2] What Jünger tries to articulate is the impact of war upon his sensibility and the implications of the war experience for post-war society and for the contemporary image of man. He does not attempt to minimize or glorify the carnage; part of his task is to depict it as dispassionately but as graphically as possible, for the horror is a measure of the test which he has to endure.

The elite Jünger describes are superbly trained beasts of prey, embodiments of the will of the nation, a new unique race of death-defying *Landsknechte*, intoxicated by danger and exhibiting a heightened vitality. Jünger invariably speaks of them in phrases redolent of Nietzsche, for they possess the characteristic combination of the Superman—ruthless courage and intelligence, animality and intellectual alertness. The theme of regression to primeval instinct with its echo of the *furor teutonicus* sounds repeatedly in Jünger's description of the psychology of the battlefield. Characteristic of this state is the complete suspension of the rational mind and the conscious will, the transcendence of individuality and a sense of being at one with the chthonic forces of existence. It is a state more akin to the Dionysian world of *The Birth of Tragedy* than to military text-books. The animal aggression, Jünger reminds us, establishes a link with the primitive phase of human culture when man moved in bands through the wilderness, constantly threatened by his environment and driven to defend himself tooth and nail. It is an orgy of the instincts recalling Freud's interpretation of the War as an inevitable deliverance from the repressive taboos of civilization. Jünger's depiction of his elite conjures up a timeless mythic image of the Warrior of whom his storm troops are but the modern embodiments. It follows that warfare is treated not as the outcome of political events

13

but as a law of nature, as basic to human existence as the sexual drive. Jünger, heir to an egregious Social Darwinism, confuses a putative aggressive instinct with its political manipulation, war.

However, Jünger is too immersed in the German intellectual tradition to forgo an Idealist transfiguration of the activities of his predatory beasts. Again and again he reminds us that their victory over self, their manly courage and determination, constitute a *spiritual* triumph. In an apotheosis of violence he describes battle as a sacred ritual, a divine judgment on two opposing ideas (put more crudely, might is right). Courage is an expression of the profound awareness that man embodies eternal, indestructible values, while a brave death demonstrates his inner nobility. The *Landsknechte* are unconscious tools of the *Weltgeist*, men at the front (we are told) are the material which the Hegelian Idea consumes for its own purpose. Invisibly connected with the great streams of vital energy, the soldiers are driven on by a higher will as the potential force of the Idea becomes actual within them. Jünger's metaphors culminate inevitably in the death wish: self-sacrifice for a conviction is man's supreme ethical accomplishment.

Clearly there is a contradiction between Jünger's primitivism, his celebration of animal instinct, and this idealistic gloss. It is difficult to reconcile obedience to a primeval blood lust with fulfilment of a spiritual imperative. Similarly there is a contradiction between the image of the elite as beasts of prey and his anachronistic references to chivalrous values. The sense of an ageless pattern of conflict is at odds with his desire to depict the horrors (and therefore the moral victories) of *this* war as unique and unprecedented. There is an unresolved tension between the reality of the war of attrition and Jünger's emphasis on the decisive importance of human qualities. And there is an uneasy marriage between Jünger's natural elitism and his wish to stress the collective unity of the *Frontgemeinschaft*, the comradeship of the front line. Behind all these, however, a more fundamental paradox can be glimpsed. Jünger's glorification of hardness, courage, and blood-lust, his search for existential validation in the jaws of death, is a desperate attempt to overcome his incipient awareness of futility and meaningless destruction. The last metaphysical activity within the framework of European nihilism is not aestheticism, as Nietzsche maintained, but Jünger's apotheosis of violence—though it might be argued that barbarity arises precisely out of the aestheticization of horror. The mythic image of the Warrior and the hypostasization of his struggle barely shroud that chilling vision of the void which Jünger was vouchsafed in the mud of

Flanders. The fear of chaos and nihilism stalks these early pages despite the defensive barriers of Idealist philosophy. The inner serenity of Idealism has become a rictus of hopelessness on the face of the living dead. To Jünger, as to his great mentor Nietzsche, history appears as a bleak vista of endless power struggles, a *perpetuum mobile*, whose futility and brutality can only be kept at bay through aesthetic transfiguration and defiant self-affirmation.

Although this is not the place to examine Jünger's career as an influential publicist or to assess his contribution to the ideology of German fascism,[3] his war books clearly raise the question of how the war experience was to inspire a restructuring of society. He felt that the war generation, an elite with a strong group consciousness moulded by common experience, had it in their power to fashion a new social order. The worship of technological production, the presumptuous belief in the power of reason and in the inevitability of progress, the cult of positivism and materialism, the notion that the scientific spirit held the key to true wisdom—these and similar nineteenth-century heresies had been belied and discredited by the War and the unleashing of atavistic passions. The War was not the end but the beginning of an age of violence. In the face of such a vision the republican world of the twenties appeared cowardly, vulgar and escapist. The pronounced fatalism with which Jünger had greeted the War as a historical event, his consistent refusal to question or even discuss the political issues at stake, lasted only as long as the authoritarian, hierarchical structure for which he had fought. During the republican years he threw himself into the political fray on the side of the extra-parliamentary opposition.[4]

When one looks at a later ideological statement such as *Die totale Mobilmachung* (1930), one sees that Jünger is still endeavouring to apply the lessons of the War to the contemporary social and political situation. His notion of total mobilization, of the harnessing of every citizen, every area of activity, to the national effort, was the corollary of the age of the masses and of advanced industrial technology, and therefore part of the ineluctable process of history. Jünger has clearly resolved some of the contradictions inherent in his earlier war books in favour of an enthusiastic affirmation of what he deems to be the dominant tendencies of the age. There remains a painful acknowledgment that the traditional heroism of the warrior-caste is redundant in an era of democratic rationalization, that the wars of knights, kings and even citizens have ceded to those of the Worker (not the economic class of Marxist definition but the anonymous, socially undifferentiated drone who exists for the purpose of maximum achievement in a totally mobilized society).

Jünger argued that socialism and nationalism were the two great mill-stones between which the vestiges of the old world were being crushed. They stood for the forces of mass organization, anonymity and con-formity, the total eclipse of individualism, and a fetishism of the machine. They would end by destroying even Progress itself—and, with a strong echo of Spengler's *Kulturpessimismus*, Jünger again be-trayed that nihilism which had confronted him in the vortex of war. The future, he predicted, would be a 'glacier world' of pain and death: it behove us to prepare for it. His attempt to conceal that icy vista in a fog of high-mindedness fails. The helpless disaffection of the new Caesars cannot identify with any existing social blueprint and their vaunted 'superfluity' of life culminates only in death.

Yet in its very febrile aimlessness this attitude was helping to forge a new reality which would be far removed from its idealistic abstractions. Jünger's concept of total mobilization is fundamentally an attempt to devise a new solution to the problems of modern industrial society as an alternative to Marxism. What in fact emerges is an ideological equivalent of economic rationalization, stamped with the hallmark of fascism. In practice it became the world of Goebbels, Himmler and Speer. When the future finally materialized, Jünger withdrew in disgust from the political scene.

2. Arnold Zweig: *Der Streit um den Sergeanten Grischa* (1927)

Of course, the overtly militarist books did not have the field to them-selves. Erich Maria Remarque's *Im Westen nichts Neues* sold far better than any single nationalist war novel. With its insistent theme of a whole generation uprooted, disillusioned and alienated by the War, it touched a profound chord in the hearts of contemporary readers. The hero Paul and his friends repudiate the Wilhelmine world and will remain as alienated from post-war civilian society as Jünger or his fellow radicals. They share with right-wing war literature the sense of regression to a more primitive state of being. But Remarque avoids any ideological extrapolation. The scene in a crater, where Paul, face to face with the Frenchman he has just killed, delivers a rhetorical set-piece on the brotherhood of man, has no practical consequences for him, and even in its formulation of the problem avoids the crux of the matter:

the social conditioning of human behaviour. The curiously illogical, conciliatory manner of Paul's timely death; the emphasis on the discomfiture of authoritarian bullies or on erotic escapades; the banality and sentimentality of the language; the absurd narrative technique involving a first-person narrator who tells his story in the historic present tense yet is dead by the end of the book; the lack of coherence and substance in the character of Paul; the contradiction between his self-conscious crudity or primitivism and his occasional non-committal ripple of humanitarian feeling—all this adds up to a true 'best seller' that confirms and affirms, but does not challenge or elucidate the readers' experience.

Another well-known war book, Ludwig Renn's *Krieg* (1928), consistently excluded any sense of self-pity. It is a laconic and detached account of the infantry war in the West, an example of unpretentious but authentic reportage. Here too the political dimension is absent, except in the rudimentary sense that Renn rejects patriotic clichés or indicates the antipathy of the fighting troops towards the revolutionaries and mutineers in the rear.[5] Hans Carossa's *Rumänisches Tagebuch* (1924) was a far more 'literary' work, full of impressionistic descriptions of sky and landscape, accounts of the author's dreams, and ethical or philosophical reflections. Its interest lies in the manner in which it shows a latter-day Idealist trying to come to terms with the War through a devalued metaphysic of nature. The inherent aestheticism springs from his inability to respond with compassion to the impact of pain, anguish and death. The narrator's sense of inner freedom is bought at the cost of empathy and involvement. It represents an avoidance, rather than a transcendence of experience. A surrogate religiosity bereft of any true object leads not to God, but back into the self. The corruption of the most important ethical precept of Idealism— the Kantian admonition that no man should serve as means to an end— manifests itself in the narrator's readiness to abstract lofty spiritual edification from the suffering of others.[6]

Zweig's novel *Der Streit um den Sergeanten Grischa* differs from the majority of German war books in being set wholly behind the lines. The author is concerned not simply with the impact of the 'storm of steel' on the individual sensibility but with the historical context in which the War was fought. Through the story of an escaped Russian prisoner who is recaptured and sentenced to death, and the people with whom he comes into contact, Zweig sets out to reveal the true social and political motives behind the War and their consequences for ordinary men. His

17

novel is a document of analysis and protest, bodied forth in the individual characters and their fate.

Though Grischa's death is morally and legally unjustified, the German High Command is determined to prevent revolutionary and pacifist ideas from infecting the Army (the year is 1917) and to this end insists on ruthless disciplinary measures. Grischa's death is a warning to defeatists, potential deserters or mutineers that the military authorities will deal implacably with any attempted defiance. Furthermore the machinery of military justice must neither admit a mistake nor exhibit leniency, for to do so would impair the respect and fear it commands. However, Grischa is also a pawn in a secondary conflict, the personal relationship between two German generals—which in turn represents a power struggle within German society. Schieffenzahn, Commander-in-Chief and a bourgeois meritocrat, has had throughout his life to pit his wits against the stupidity and arrogance of higher-born comrades. Confronted with von Lychow, the local divisional commander who protests against the death-sentence, he sees himself once again face to face with the old feudal traditions, the narrow-minded *Junkertum* that is inimical to the new, technologically rationalized society of Wilhelmine Germany. A class score is settled—and Grischa dies.

The political ambitions of this new Germany are made clear enough. They involve the acquisition of vast territorial gains in the East. The German people are predestined to play a role of conquest and world domination that is only just beginning. But who are the German 'people'? It is equally clear that these expansionist dreams belong to the ruling class of militarists and industrialists, and to the bourgeois managers and civil servants who live comfortably off the misfortunes of others. There is a parallel between their pursuit of territorial gains and their social dominance in pre-war Germany; they will rule the new subject peoples with the ruthless determination which they showed towards the German working class up to 1914 and especially from that fateful summer onwards. Thus the machinery of German militarism in which Grischa is enmeshed is linked to the social structure of a Germany divided into exploiters and exploited. Instead of the division between the two nations, the front line and the civilian population at home, which figures frequently in nationalist war books, Zweig presents us with a different tension—the social gulf between officers and men, a leitmotif of German anti-war literature.

Lest the picture appear too simplified, however, Zweig supplies differentiated portraits of individual members of the officer class in such a way that those who still preserve some vestiges of decency and compassion are seen to be no less imprisoned by the system than Grischa or any other common soldier. Conversely, the theme of working-class solidarity, central to Communist writing, is treated in a realistic fashion. Fellow-feeling cannot break the compulsive hold of discipline and overcome the fear of retaliation. Only in the closing pages of the novel does the theme of comradeship sound a triumphantly sentimental note. The political corollary is then suggested: the working class whose cooperation is essential to the prosecution of modern warfare also have it in their power to bring the War to an end.

The tendentious nature of Zweig's book is not in dispute. What is remarkable, however, is the extensive historical analysis which he manages to integrate into the story of a relatively obscure character, and the objectivity with which he presents a wide spectrum of social allegiance and political opinion. Nowhere is this objectivity more evident than in the portrait of von Lychow, who grows in stature as the novel proceeds, without being able to transcend the limitations of his background.

If the strength of Zweig's novel lies in its depiction of various reactions to Grischa's dilemma with their intermingling of private, social and political factors, its main weakness lies in the portrait of Grischa himself. He is too much the amiable, sympathetic, unwitting victim, too literary a creation altogether for the Russian peasant he is supposed to be. This is well attested in the dream which he has on the eve of his execution and through which he achieves a measure of acquiescence in his death. He sees it as an atonement for the blood he himself has shed earlier in the War as an ordinary soldier. Leaving aside the sophisticated sequence of images and the highly articulate consciousness revealed here, one cannot help querying the propriety of this religious insight in a novel predominantly concerned with political realities. The logic of Grischa's dream is that he deserves to die. But this is at odds with the message of the novel as a whole. Zweig does not distinguish carefully enough between Grischa's subjective religious acceptance of his impending execution and the need to indict the social evil which it epitomizes.

Der Streit um den Sergeanten Grischa remains one of the most sober and wide-ranging of German war novels. It eschews the abstract idealism of the pacifist writing of the Expressionists. It is alive to the suffering of individuals but sets this in a historical context. It succeeds in conveying a poignant sense of the diminishment which Grischa's death inflicts upon his fellows, and intimates the richness and abundant sweetness which life might have held for him. Here at least the realism of the novel does not falter. (Compare the contemptuous abstractions of Jünger, his disparagement and repudiation of compassion and love.)[7] Above all it manages to convey the corruption and inhumanity of a social system which inhibits a man's best instincts and treats individuals as means not ends.

From his combination of social analysis and humanitarian protest Zweig was eventually to move into the Marxist camp. He continued to write in a social-realist mode and slowly completed a whole cycle of novels depicting the First World War as the cataclysm of bourgeois civilization.[8]

Chapter Two
The Literature of Revolution

A. Expressionism

Like the political revolution to which it ran parallel, the literary revolution of Expressionism had its roots in the pre-war period.[1] And like the political upheavals of 1918–19 it was given a decisive impetus by the War. The Russian Revolution of 1917 had little immediate impact on German writers opposed to the Imperial regime but the November Revolution in Germany itself inspired an upsurge of literary commitment. Early Expressionism had, it is true, sometimes produced a poetry of social protest but the commitment of a man like Franz Pfemfert, editor of one of the leading Expressionist periodicals *Die Aktion,* was shared by few members of the younger literary generation before the War. *Die Aktion* kept up its political criticisms during the War within the narrow limits allowed by censorship. The political comment was often implicit and indirect, achieved for instance by the publication of the war poems of serving soldiers or by the reprinting of texts by French and Russian writers that intimated a common experience. From April 1915 Pfemfert regularly published extracts from the press and current publications, demonstrating without comment the inhumanity of the pro-war faction. (No gloss was needed in the context of *Die Aktion* whose editorial values were already familiar.) *Die Aktion* also supplied reports on the course of the Russian Revolution. Another widely circulated Expressionist periodical *Die weissen Blätter* remained mainly literary even after its move to neutral Switzerland in 1916, but it did print occasional anti-war pieces by Leonhard Frank, Becher, Barbusse, Rolland and others. Whereas Pfemfert saw the War as a political event, *Die weissen Blätter* inclined towards a historical fatalism, regarding the War as the inevitable crisis of technological civilization out of which some new world would dawn.

By the end of the War the political activism of the 'rhetorical' Expressionists was gathering momentum. This second phase was relatively homogeneous in its ambitions and techniques. The Expressionists repudiated the bourgeois world of their parents with its ruthless economic doctrine, its obsessive materialism and its aggressive individualism. They threw off the shackles of nineteenth-century determinism, whether sociological or biological, and condemned the shallow rationalism of the old world. They sought to penetrate to the essence of reality and to articulate an intuitive vision of the Idea. They cultivated emotion, intoxication, ecstasy as the means of experiencing noumenal truths and of establishing a link with cosmic forces. Imbued with religious, even Messianic zeal, they created universal patterns of experience and archetypal figures, abandoning psychology for mythic abstractions, the better to release the Spirit from the vessel of the phenomenal world. In all this the Expressionists reveal a curious affinity with the conservative or conservative-revolutionary response to the War such as can be seen in Carossa or Jünger. Where 'rhetorical' Expressionism differs from conservative idealism is in its activist impulse to change the world. Where it contrasts with the national revolutionaries is in its humanist compassion and faith in universal brotherhood, though its religious emotionalism is not without a certain moral ambivalence. Expressionism posits the transformation of the individual soul as a prerequisite of the transformation of human society and accordingly preaches a Tolstoyan gospel of love and peace. Here for the first time German Idealism found itself actively involved in a revolutionary situation.[2] The story of that involvement is also the story of the limitations of the tradition itself when faced with the challenge of social change.

The Expressionist endeavour to unleash a spiritual and moral revolution was accompanied by the exploding of conventional literary forms and techniques. A dynamic vocabulary, a convulsive paratactic syntax in which ideas followed one upon the other without logical connections; rhetorical inversions; repetition and accumulation; the isolation of key words for emphasis; the omission of articles and inflexions; ellipsis and condensation—these were some of the linguistic features manipulated by the Expressionists to sustain a mood of rhapsodic intensity and to assault the emotions of the reader or audience. In the theatre, light and sound effects were exploited to reinforce dream-like (or nightmarish) visions and to impart a breath of infinity; geometric and abstract designs universalized the settings and heightened the emotional impact; and a deliberately 'theatrical', declamatory style of acting aimed at sweeping the audience off its feet, overwhelmed by the power of a spiritual experience. The dramatic structure abandoned along with psychology and dialogue the notion of a plot and a carefully integrated development: the characteristic pattern was a series of almost autonomous scenes, each marking a significant 'station' on the hero's road to sacrifice and fulfilment. Expressionist drama depicted not reality but the image of reality in the mind of the subject.[3] Consequently there was no room for dramatic irony, merely for a series of revelations. In fact the stage was invaded by fundamentally undramatic qualities,[4] conducive not of character portrayal but of typological abstractions, not of dialogue but of declamation, not of action and conflict but of a predetermined irresistible attraction towards the magnetic pole of spirit.

When the Expressionist generation threw itself into political activism, it opted for emotional impact and immediacy both in the genres it favoured and in its relationship with its public. The novel was neglected in favour of poetry, the drama of prophecy and revelation flourished, and public readings vied with little magazines, pamphlets and brochures as the most popular outlet for Messianic fervour. The aesthetic experience was seen as a ritual of conversion and dedication, prior to a direct attack on reality. Expressionist writers did not attempt to argue, define or convince: they launched key words and slogans at their audiences in a bid to suspend rational thought and impart a religious enthusiasm. It has been rightly observed that the core of Expressionist writing, even when it attempted to grapple with social and political issues, remained 'a personal religious transformation'.[5]

In all this the Expressionists anticipated the emotional impulses which would be exploited and manipulated by National Socialism. Their intense willingness for self-sacrifice, their ecstasy in suffering, their powerful sense of community, and their experience of mystical inspiration sprang from a belief in sublime radicalism as an end in itself. Though the circumstances of the religious experience might be questionable and the consequences of these emotions catastrophic, the Messianic drive was self-justifying. There was a danger of the symbolic dramatic action ceding to an appeal for a more literal imitation of the sacrificial mode: Hanns Johst's *Schlageter* (1933), a play commemorating one of the early Nazi 'martyrs', bears the hallmark of its author's Expressionist origins, with its quasi-religious vocabulary of the Passion, a faith unto death, a service which is its own reward, a love which atones for all errors—and its final ecstatic summons to Germany to erupt into a cleansing conflagration. Heyricke's *Neurode* or Richard Euringer's *Deutsche Passion 1933*, featuring the Unknown Soldier as a Christ figure, likewise demonstrate the transition from ethical abstractions to fanatical commitment. The true precedents for this fatal confusion of ethical imperatives, social radicalism and apocalyptic criminality are the millenarian movements of the Middle Ages; its heirs are the myrmidons of the new millennium proclaimed in 1933.[6]

Inevitably the febrile atmosphere of the Expressionist era, the opportunities for self-exposure, the unfocused abstractions and the primacy of feeling encouraged a degeneration into mannerism and emotional cliché. Subjectivism declined all too easily into exhibitionism and self-deification, and this crisis itself became an excuse for endless self-analysis. The conflict between the generations released too much uncontrolled adolescent vitality, while the liberation of poetic form rapidly turned into anarchic licence. As the social world proved intractable to the voice of the Spirit and the emotional intensity was dissipated, Expressionist idealism rallied briefly in an inverted form to bury its old hopes beneath a layer of sadistic cruelty and animal vitalism, and a welter of scatological imagery. But by about 1924 even this satanic impulse was spent, and the murky metaphysics was assimilated to more timely radicalisms.

The 'rhetorical' Expressionists spurned conventional political routine and the existing parties. Their sympathies were with the Left but their idealism tempted them into trying to vault over the area of political organization altogether. Their image of man deliberately erased the influence of social forces to which the individual is subject in the modern world and their utopianism thus amounted to little more than a whistling in the dark. One of the rare instances of an attempt to grapple with particular social problems can be seen in the *Aktivismus* group led by Kurt Hiller whose quixotic blend of social reforms, private obsessions and unabashed elitism met with short shrift from the revolutionary workers of Berlin.[7]

The pattern of enthusiasm and bitter disenchantment that marks Hiller's Activism likewise informs the contemporary trilogy by Georg Kaiser, one of the best known dramatists of his generation. The plays bear the titles *Die Koralle*, *Gas I* and *Gas II*. The action is characteristically remote from the concrete revolutionary situation, while yet presenting symbolic parallels to the crisis of capitalism and the war of attrition, and offering a challenge to create a new Heaven and a new Earth. What is interesting here is not merely the indictment of an inhumane civilization or the acknowledgment that the New Man has been repudiated like the first Messiah; we witness too the helplessness of a reformer who perceives the evils of economic rationalization and alienation without being able to offer any alternative other than 'three acres and a cow' or a withdrawal into inwardness. The dilemma is not Kaiser's alone but that of Expressionist idealism in general. Equally significant is the chiliastic zeal with which the hero of *Gas II* destroys his fellow workers for the good of their souls, casting aside all immediate moral responsibility in his thirst to achieve an untrammelled victory for the principle he represents.

Ernst Toller: *Die Wandlung* (1917–18) and *Masse-Mensch* (1919)

Of all the Expressionist writers Ernst Toller was the one most deeply enmeshed in practical politics.[8] While his early work manifests many of the characteristic features of 'rhetorical' Expressionism, it has the advantage of being moulded by first-hand experience of a revolutionary situation. In November 1918 Toller was one of the intellectuals who played a leading part in the short-lived socialist revolution in Munich (where Gustav Landauer and Erich Mühsam were among his colleagues). Subsequently Toller spent five years in prison for high treason.

His play *Die Wandlung* (written 1917–18), subtitled 'Das Ringen eines Menschen', belongs to the optimistic, enthusiastic phase of Expressionism. It depicts the development of the hero from a confused, alienated outsider to the status of a redeeming prophet. The emphasis lies on his individual purification and spiritual fulfilment—the extension of this into the social world takes place not in a historical situation but in a solipsistic wish-dream. Ushered in by a surrealist attack on the German war machine, the play articulates the vibrant hope of the 'rhetorical' Expressionists that out of the feast of death and horror a regenerated humanity would emerge. A febrile intensity and a breathless sequence of images, nightmarish or transfigured, sustain the drama, which is divided into 'stations' alternating between relatively realistic scenes played front-stage, and shadowy, dream-like inserts enacted at the rear of the stage. The spectral scenes counterpoint Friedrich's experience in the social world, showing the reality beneath the clichés and deceptions of bourgeois civilization.

In the final scene Friedrich delivers a long exhortation, urging that spiritual renewal must precede social upheaval; any change in the social world must be effected in a spirit of love and forgiveness. And he concludes on a note of millennial optimism, with a direct appeal to his audience in the spirit of 'rhetorical' Expressionism. (So too Walter

25

Hasenclever's *Antigone* (1917) had ended with the heroine's voice calling from the grave to urge prayer, atonement and forgiveness instead of violent retribution.)[9] When (to adapt Friedrich's peroration) the powers that be proved deaf to the 'organ voluntaries' of the masses, when the soldiers turned their swords on the revolution instead of turning them into ploughshares, when the citadels were found to be made of stone not of brittle slack, the Expressionist fervour collapsed. Its influence survived only as an aesthetic and emotional legacy. As Brecht sardonically commented, it freed itself only from grammatical rules, not from the toils of capitalism.[10]

After the defeat of the revolution Toller became a critical socialist whose ethical idealism was tempered by a realistic awareness of the problems and limitations of political activity. His play *Masse-Mensch* records an early stage in this process, when he faces up to the problem of violence and the relationship between means and ends. With memories behind him of the conflict between moderate and extremist revolutionaries in Munich, and having experienced himself the savage retaliation of the reactionary regime, Toller tries to articulate the dilemma and the tragic alternatives facing those who would destroy a corrupt but still powerful social order. The form, the style and the intensity of the play are still characteristic of 'rhetorical' Expressionism. The insight which the play affords, however, goes far beyond the attitudes of most of Toller's Expressionist contemporaries and his own earlier position. Here the conflict is not so much between the old world and the new as between two opposing ideas of change, as embodied in the Woman who clings to her humanist principles, and the anonymous agitator who believes in the necessity for ruthless revolutionary violence. Do the ends justify the means? Is the agitator any better than the system he attempts to destroy? Can the idealist impetus of revolution survive a recourse to violence? Can the established order be defeated in any other way? Can might and right be reconciled? Can future gain be purchased at the price of present loss? The Woman remains true to an idealism which refuses to reduce individuals to means and will not countenance bloodshed for the sake of the cause she believes in. The agitator remains relentlessly pragmatic. There is no compromise, no resolution. The Woman fails to persuade the world to accept her values and can only be effective as a martyr of the revolution she deplored, with the blood of innocent victims on her hands. In order to alleviate the impact of this tragic dilemma, the ending diverts our attention from the issue of political morality to the tentative hope of personal contrition and regeneration, a shift from the political to the religious plane which betokens the failure of Idealism to come to terms with revolutionary activism.

B. Proletarian Literature

One of the major tasks confronting left-wing writers during the Weimar years was the need to develop their own distinctive art forms in the struggle against capitalism and fascism.[11] When in 1925, after a period of fragmentation and disarray among left-wing factions, the German Communist Party emerged as the sole revolutionary alternative to the Social Democrats, it had no official aesthetic doctrine, except in so far as the reviews in the Party newspaper *Die Rote Fahne* had shown a high regard for the bourgeois classics of the eighteenth and nineteenth centuries and a negative attitude towards aesthetic modernism. Indeed the KPD was suspicious of literary activity altogether on the grounds that it was ineffective and superfluous. Writers were welcomed purely as agents of propaganda of the crudest kind, pending the successful revolution which would lay the foundation of a truly proletarian culture. But the translation in 1924 of Lenin's *Party Organisation and Party Literature* and the 'Bolshevization' of the German Party in the mid-twenties did set in train a theoretical discussion of the tasks facing the Communist writer.

The general aims of Communist writing were to create a literature which satisfied the reading needs of the proletariat, revealed to it the truth about capitalist society and reinforced its class consciousness. Such a literature had a paramount didactic purpose: to mobilize the masses for the class struggle, but it also had a cultural aim, the combatting of the conservative, even philistine artistic tastes of the working class as mirrored in its preference for the sentimental trash which poured from the bourgeois presses of Ullstein and Scherl in cheap editions. There remained, however, the basic problem of defining the nature of 'proletarian' literature. Was it something written by or for the working class—or both? Should it employ new forms or merely new subjects—or both? Should it confine itself to the conditions and experience of the proletariat? Or should it take a wider view, retaining a revolutionary perspective on society? What is clear is that by the late twenties 'proletarian' literature was generally thought to be determined not so much by the class origins of the writer as by his philosophical and political commitment. On the other hand, there was still a strong tendency to favour working-class authors. Proletarian writers were seen as the main reservoir of socialist art. Workers were encouraged to try their hand at writing, first through short reports or personal accounts for the Party organs, then progressing to short fictional forms (the 'worker-correspondents' movement sanctioned by Lenin and Sinovjev). Working-class theatre groups were also active, devising their own agitatory material. In 1930 the 'Roter Eine-Mark-Roman' was launched, a series of novels written by working-class authors for the masses and depicting the life of the proletariat in factories, mines, tenements or on the barricades. The first titles included Hans Marchwitza's *Sturm auf Essen*, Klaus Neukrantz's *Barrikaden am Wedding* and Willi Bredel's *Maschinenfabrik N. und K.* Like the fully fledged 'socialist realism' of which these books were harbingers, the ostensible endeavour was 'to gain and make meaningful for literature the area of workaday life which bourgeois realism' had neglected. But the attempt was frustrated from the start by the stereotyped ideological patterns, the predictable, over-simplified evaluations and impoverished clichéd language.[12]

In 1928 a major organizational development occurred with the founding of the *Bund proletarisch-revolutionärer Schriftsteller* to co-ordinate the literary offensive of the KPD. Its programme was based on the Soviet WAPP programme of 1924 and its activities were funded direct from Moscow. Initially it considered the value of progressive bourgeois allies—that is, middle-class intellectuals who had joined the Party or who supported the Communist cause—to lie in their ability to play midwife to the nascent creative talents of the proletariat.

These early attempts to reconcile the demands of agitation, diversion and literary ambition proved disappointing. Johannes R. Becher, as editor of the *Linkskurve*, the official journal of the BPRS, urged writers to turn to pamphleteering as a more useful application of their talents. Other voices indicated the need to evolve a revolutionary aesthetic form corresponding to the revolutionary political message that it was intended to convey. The dramatist Berta Lask argued the case for moving away from the individualism of bourgeois literature towards a sense of the collective; such a change might involve mass dramas, revues and choral recitation. The individual character should be presented not as an autonomous personality but as an exponent of the historical role of his class. (Her own plays, e.g., *Thomas Münzer* [1925] and *Leuna 1921* [1927], depicted events in the history of the working-class movement, using huge casts and epic spectacles under the influence of the *proletkult* and Meyerhold.)[13] In 1930 the 'proletarian novel' was the theme of a radio discussion between the German-speaking Czech Communist F. C. Weiskopf and Kurt Hirschfeld. Weiskopf could do no more than aver that the genre was still in a formative stage. The features it would display included an emphasis on collective action and collective feeling, and the extension of the boundaries of fictional form to include reportage and the chronicle style. The language of the 'proletarian novel' would need to encompass the vocabulary of the political and trade union movement, the vernacular of the cities and the shop-floor. If such suggestions were still little more than crudely tentative, more cogent and forceful ideas were being advanced by Brecht whose 'epic' theatre envisaged a form that broke with nineteenth-century bourgeois drama in order to meet the changing needs of an age of revolution.

By the beginning of the thirties a rift was evident between the 'modernist' writers who were seeking new forms, and the conservatives who were beginning to follow the increasingly intolerant and traditionalist Moscow line. Their dissension illustrated the wider political problem of a German Communist Party which had come to be dominated by Soviet-inspired policies often at odds with conditions in Germany. On the one hand Becher, Andor Gábor, Alfred Kurella and Georg Lukács, the controlling voices in the BPRS and the *Linkskurve*, moved in the direction of socialist realism. On the other hand Brecht, Walter Benjamin, Hanns Eisler and Ernst Bloch advocated more progressive forms. Lukács argued that modernist experiment was the expression of a decadent bourgeoisie. The burden of the radical position was that form was determined by the technical possibilities of communication and reproduction, and by the changing structure and needs of the audience. But Lukács insistently advocated the combination of a Tolstoyan totality and breadth with a Marxist analysis of society. His conservative aesthetic paradoxically abandoned immediate political impact for the sake of a higher task, the creation of the great proletarian work of art. Although Lukács attacked the avant-garde deviationists, he never quite became a proponent of socialist realism as taught by Zhdanov, with its deliberate mixture of description and prescription and its singular lack of objectivity. The critical debate was to continue even after 1933, notably in the public exchange of letters between Lukács and Anna Seghers over the problem of realism, and in the arguments about Expressionism.[14]

Within the KPD it was the conservative line that triumphed. In 1935 the KPD declared the need to mobilize the 'classical' bourgeois heritage in the struggle against fascism. One of the curious results of the conservative victory was that the highly 'bourgeois' and self-consciously modernist novels of Thomas Mann were hailed as prototypes of the new realism, while the aims of Brecht and his associates were denounced as decadent and formalistic. The BPRS ended by advocating a novel of milieu concerned with all the groups and tendencies within the working class and the lower middle class. Such a literature would extend the nineteenth-century realist tradition and was (in theory) to be committed without being crudely didactic. It would reject the idea of a collective literature where the masses themselves became the protagonist, preferring the use of representative individuals. It would avoid the overt intervention of the author or narrator. The conservative line similarly attacked the documentary principle, the use of reportage and all 'naturalism', advocating instead character portrayal and psychological interest. Mimesis triumphed over demonstration, illusion and empathy over cool appraisal, a would-be total view over the instructive singular example.

When one surveys the products of left-wing writing in Germany between the wars, it seems that the only successful importation from the Soviet Union was the idea of agitprop theatre. Here it was a case not of literary achievement but of public rituals designed to confirm and strengthen political resolve. The merits of agitprop lay not in any text, for it aimed at the obliteration of art forms other than the cartoon, the sketch and the poster, but in the collective experience and revolutionary fervour it inspired. It preached to the converted, and bored or infuriated the rest. A significant feature of the Socialist theatre of the twenties was the *Sprechchor* movement. Ernst Toller was among the first dramatists to write choral works for amateur performance—'semi-dramatic compositions with spoken parts for individual voices, groups and full chorus, recited to musical accompaniment'.[15] Toller also wrote for trade-union festivals so-called *Massenfestspiele*, scenarios or pageants that were performed outdoors by enormous casts. Brecht's own *Lehrstücke*, the didactic plays of the late twenties and early thirties, are rooted in this workers' theatre.[16]

The commercial pendant to the workers' pageants, parables, choral works, revues and Marxist morality plays was to be found in the theatre of Erwin Piscator.[17] Piscator too was anxious to find alternatives to the individualist literature of the bourgeoisie. But he was not content merely to depict man in the mass in order to show that an individual fate was shared by thousands. Rather, he set out to reveal the social and economic causes which turned individual conflict into class conflict. Drama, he believed, should reach out beyond the confines of the stage and establish direct links with social reality by documentary methods. Piscator had already presented early agitprop pieces in Berlin with amateur casts. In the mid-twenties he put together two revues, *Revue Roter Rummel* (1924) and *Trotz Alledem!* (1925), which became models for many subsequent agitprop productions. Indeed the revue form replaced the mass spectacles and choral works as the favourite vehicle of workers' theatre groups. This tendency was reinforced by a visit to Germany in 1927 of a Moscow troupe specializing in the 'Living Newspaper' technique. Through music, mime and dance they enacted and interpreted items of current news. In 1929 there were 180 agitprop groups in Germany with a potential audience of three and a half million. The limitations of the agitprop tradition were, of course, its built-in obsolescence.[18]

From 1927 Piscator relinquished agitprop in favour of an attempt to revolutionize the conventional theatre—an attempt in which the technical resources of the stage were to be of supreme importance as befitted the age of technology. Piscator emphasized the economic and social background of the action at the expense of character. He emphasized visual impact over the spoken word. He emphasized mechanics over acting and dialogue, frequently overreaching his resources in the process. He used captions, exposed the stage machinery, utilized narrator figures who commented on events and addressed the audience, introduced film and documentary material. There was no attempt at creating any illusion of reality on stage: events were self-consciously enacted. Props were used to supply information, not to reinforce illusion. Yet Piscator still endeavoured to involve his audience totally in the theatrical experience, therein marking a crucial distinction between his ideas and those of Brecht's 'epic' theatre.

1. Friedrich Wolf: *Die Matrosen von Cattaro* (1930)

Discontent and rebellion in the Imperial Navy had been an important factor in the revolutionary upheavals of 1918. As the War entered its fourth year, sporadic outbursts of unrest heralded the coming storm. During the later Weimar period the sailors who had been savagely punished for their part in the initial unsuccessful mutinies figured in several works by left-wing writers, where they were accorded a martyr's status similar to that given to the *communards* of 1871 or the Russian revolutionaries of 1905. Theodor Plivier's reportage-novel *Des Kaisers Kulis* and Toller's documentary drama *Feuer aus den Kesseln* both dealt with a mutiny in the German fleet in 1917 after which the ringleaders had been shot. Piscator dramatized Plivier's story. And Friedrich Wolf, after a number of social plays, turned for his next subject to the mutiny in the Austro-Hungarian navy at Cattaro early in 1918. Whereas Plivier and Toller were both concerned to attack the system against which the mutineers had rebelled (a system whose spirit survived in nationalist circles) and to commemorate their sacrifice, Wolf went a stage further. His drama sought to teach a lesson by exposing the fatal errors of the naval mutineers and drawing explicit consequences from their defeat. As a writer firmly committed to the KPD line and to the agitatory function of art, Wolf treated his subject in an openly didactic fashion. Plivier, who was not a Party member and was in fact considered an anarchist by the Marxist–Leninists, attempted to reproduce the total wartime experience of the German sailor in the objectivist mode. Toller for his part tried to explain how and why the mutiny occurred and to attack the real offenders. Wolf compressed the underlying causes of the Cattaro revolt into a documentary preface listing the men's grievances as confirmed by an official enquiry of the time. His play opens on the very eve of the mutiny. Not the causes but the results are at the centre of his intention: *Die Matrosen von Cattaro* is an object lesson in Leninist tactics.

2. Anna Seghers: *Die Gefährten* (1932)

It was not easy for the KPD to find writers who could combine a correct ideological attitude with a degree of creative ability. Many of the writers sympathetic to the socialist cause avoided presenting the Party's policies or its activities in a direct fashion. Plivier's account of the German Fleet dealt with figures who were not politically organized. Renn's *Krieg* spurned political discussion altogether. Anna Segher's prize-winning *Aufstand der Fischer von St Barbara* depicted (before she joined the Party) a forlorn rebellion and an almost existentialist hero in a manner far removed from the notion of art as a 'searchlight' or 'weapon'. Brecht, it is true, set out to draw a revolutionary moral from a picture of the Party at work in *Die Massnahme* but thereby failed to satisfy the orthodox Party critics. The majority of his didactic plays are moral parables abstracted from a concrete political situation. Only in one play —his adaptation of Gorki's *The Mother*—did he show the development of a revolutionary consciousness culminating in commitment to the Party (and there he chose a context at several removes from the ideological or tactical debates of the Weimar years). Among the targets of orthodox critics were books in which the workers appeared as a sullen mass, crippled by exploitation and erupting in futile rebellion (e.g., Wolf's novel *Kreatur* of 1926); works which showed the proletariat dependent upon bourgeois leaders for positive direction (e.g., Wolf's play *Kolonne Hund* of 1927); and writers such as Plivier who supported the theory of spontaneous rebellion and misconstrued the role of the Party in its relationship to the workers.[19] Anna Segher's novel *Die Gefährten* which was intended to depict the anti-fascist struggle of a hydra-headed Party in many European countries represented something of an exception in its immediate depiction of the current situation and its stress on Communist organization and agitation. Yet the novel contains significant omissions. There are no discussions of ideology, merely the portrayal of attitudes towards it. There is no critical attempt to get to the bottom of the contemporary position of the Party, but only a series of tributes to the courage and tenacity of those who fight for the cause. And although many of the characters visit the Soviet Union, although several of them live in Germany, there is no analysis of the problems and difficulties facing the Soviet Party or the KPD: in other words the Party in power or the Party in legal opposition within a parliamentary framework. Segher's attention focuses on those countries such as Hungary or Bulgaria where the Party must work clandestinely and where the mere problem of survival obviates the need to consider present tactics or ultimate purposes.

In *Die Gefährten* the novelist attempted to write a fictional work that departed from conventional realism, above all a work which reproduced that sense of collective experience often mentioned as characteristic of the proletarian work of art. The novel is anti-individualist in both its theme and its form. It traces the story of numerous Communist agitators and organizers from the collapse of the Hungarian revolution in 1919 to a point later in the twenties. The scene shifts between Hungary, Poland, Italy, Russia, Germany, Bulgaria, France and China. The novel rarely devotes more than a few pages at a time to any one character before cross-cutting to another. This episodic structure is designed to preserve a sense of the myriad ramifications of Party activity and to inhibit emotional involvement on the part of the reader. In short, it is an attempt to evolve a fictional equivalent to Brecht's 'epic' theatre, albeit perhaps too mechanically conceived. Our attention is firmly fixed on the political attitudes and activities of the characters: personal relationships and emotions impinge upon the novel only in so far as they issue from or affect political behaviour. The theme of forsaking one's family (Matthew x.37) is only one of several religious motifs and images in the story. There is little psychological discrimination between the various characters, while the episodic structure often omits narrative links and explanations of cause and effect. This ellipsis extends even to the style itself, lending it greater tension and imaginative interest than will be the case in Segher's later novels which revert to more conventional techniques of realism.

3. Bertolt Brecht: *Die Massnahme* (1930)

The anti-individualism of Segher's novel, together with the revolutionary didacticism of Wolf's play, are both to the fore in Brecht's drama *Die Massnahme*. It tells of a group of Communist agitators who have just returned from a mission to China and who now explain through a series of re-enactments how they were forced to eliminate a young comrade in order to safeguard the success of their mission. As in Toller's *Masse-Mensch*, the conflict is between the emotional humanitarianism of the individualist and the unremitting logic of the faceless revolutionaries who know no loyalty except to the Party.

The structure of the play is neatly symmetrical. In each episode a preliminary narration introduces the scene and this is rounded off by a brief discussion between the agitators and the tribunal on the moral to be drawn from the preceding incident. The young comrade is criticized for separating *Gefühl* and *Verstand*, for surrendering to righteous indignation, for seeking to preserve his moral integrity and for placing his own emotional fulfilment before the long-term success of the movement. He tries to alleviate present misery or to effect superficial amelioration instead of working determinedly, clandestinely and detachedly for the transformation of the whole system. He cannot—ultimately—bring himself to sacrifice the present for the sake of the future. His reluctance to compromise himself morally, to dissimulate, to lie, to suppress his instinctive compassion will prevent him from ever helping to destroy a system which is itself completely ruthless and unscrupulous.

Commentators on *Die Massnahme* are inclined to reduce the point at issue to the conflict between emotion and reason, and the repugnant political conclusions of the piece. But surely the play indicates that intellect and feeling must be effectively combined if there is to be any real chance of changing a violent and corrupt world. The final lines do not condemn emotion as such: they accord certain productive feelings a proper place in the revolutionary attitude—but also stress the need for adequate understanding of social mechanisms and for infinite patience. Moreover the decision to eliminate the young comrade is neither unfeeling nor taken lightly. '*Furchtbar ist es, zu töten*' are the only words in the text which Brecht italicizes. There is even a gesture of *Freundlichkeit*, that supreme Brechtian virtue, in the comfort they give the young comrade at the end when they cradle his head in their arms. Yet the glib acquiescence arouses suspicion: perhaps the case is too neatly presented, the structure too symmetrical, the language too carefully constructed. By anticipating the audience's reservations and seeking to meet them in advance, by systematically dismissing all logical alternatives to the measures taken, the play impels the critical observer to resent this preemption of his judgment and to take stubborn issue with the arguments put forward, even to the point of defending the ostensibly illogical solution which would be no less credible as a political response to the dilemma. Not until a decade or more later would Brecht's imaginative writing betray the poignant sense of moral diminution occasioned by his assent to violence. Even now he does not seek to glorify violence or to transfer the responsibility to some indefinable metaphysical instance, after the manner of the right-wing radicals. His acceptance of the logic of revolution involved a strenuous effort to face up to the world as it was.

The anti-individualist theme of the play determines its techniques, such as the symbolic use of masks or the collective voice of the control-chorus representing a tribunal of the movement. The agitators (one of them a woman) take it in turns to play the role of the young comrade and to act the parts of all the other characters in the reconstructed scenes, a highly theatrical way of demonstrating that they have no fixed private personalities any more and are completely *disponible*, at the behest of the Party. But this role-playing is also an important element in the technique of 'alienation', the critical distancing of the audience from the dramatic events. Not the characters themselves as individuals but their story (and what we should learn from it) occupy our attention. The task of the 'epic' theatre is not to involve but to demonstrate. Hence the play-within-a-play which presents events at several removes. Hence the analytical discussions at the end of each episode, hence the narration which sets the scene, hence too the use of songs to interrupt the action and comment on the issues involved. Such a structure, together with the impersonal, reflective, stylized language, is designed to encourage cool appraisal and lucid thinking on the part of the audience.

Yet the play does not always maintain this atmosphere of detachment and intellectuality. The almost religious praise of the Party, for example, smacks more of the over-zealous convert than of analytical reason. It is here that the truly 'Stalinist' aspects of the play lie, in the stress on the infallibility of the Party, in the idea of being re-united with the Party by accepting guilt and expiation, in the self-indictment of the sinner, and in the determined avoidance of tragedy through the resolution of all conflicts within the Party—the Party being somehow free from the contradictions and antagonisms that otherwise dominate historical development. Brecht, of course, was not alone in his obeisance. From Ernst Fischer's retrospective account of his own experiences in Moscow in the late thirties, we gain a pertinent insight into the stratagems devised by the intellectual who, for the sake of the cause he passionately believes in, deliberately renounces scepticism, individualism and critical reason in favour of conformity and discipline. Fischer's words are equally applicable to the Brecht of the *Lehrstücke*:

> . . . he is forever calling himself to heel in the name of the collective to which he belongs and yet, in his critical self-assertion, does not belong to fully. His consciousness tells him that he is imperfectly aligned and his conscience reproaches him for it, a conscience that has not been forced upon him but was born of his own free decision, and the more refractory the rebellion of the primary, anarchic self, this irrepressible *no* of the consenting intellectual, the more vehement, out of his self-imposed conformity, will be his defence of discipline—that to him so antipathetic discipline—against insubordination, against the heretic that is himself.[20]

The notion of heresy, like the religious imagery of *Die Massnahme*, hints that the *sacrificium intellectus* was due to more than mere self-discipline. The surrogate creed which Brecht professes in his *Lehrstück* has its parallels with the debased religious longings voiced by Expressionism and later exploited by National Socialism. It is ultimately a question of what Nietzsche had called the 'instinct of weakness', the desperate need for faith, certitude and authoritative guidance, whereby the only kind of self-assertion still felt to be possible is fanatical dedication to a self-proclaimed ideal. (In Brecht's first play *Baal* metaphysical rebellion still had the courage of its anarchic, vitalist convictions.)[21]

After 1933 Brecht's ideas about the relationship between politics and literature grew more complex. His view of human character and its role in drama likewise became less simplified. The technique of *Verfremdung* was further developed and refined. Other things, however, remained constant. Brecht continued to attack bourgeois morality as a weapon in the class war. He never doubted the argument that violence could only be defeated by violence, or that the end justified the means. Even through the worst excesses of Stalinism, both in the Soviet Union and in Ulbricht's Germany—despite the Moscow trials, the Nazi-Soviet pact and the events of 1953 and 1956—he never acknowledged publicly the possibility that the means might corrupt the ends to the extent of rendering them unattainable.

C. Towards the National Revolution

1. Hans Grimm: *Volk ohne Raum* (1926)

The popularity of war literature and *Heimatromane* in the closing years of the Weimar Republic and in the Third Reich has already been mentioned. Perhaps it was because Grimm's novel managed to combine elements of both that it made such a mark on the German reading public. By 1940, despite its enormous bulk, it had sold almost half a million copies.[22] Its interest for us lies in the fact that it provides an illuminating index of the confusions besetting German conservatism in the twenties, of the degeneration of provincial literature into *völkisch* obsessions, and of the relationship between imperialist expansion and petit bourgeois resentment.

Volk ohne Raum is the major novel of German colonialism. It traces the fortunes of Cornelius Friebott from his village in Lower Saxony to the farm lands of German South-West Africa in the years between 1887 and the Weimar Republic. And it attempts to explain all the social and political problems of those years as the product of the lack of *Raum*, or 'living space' as the notion later became familiar.

The novel's criticisms of industrial Germany run parallel to many a socialist analysis and for a time the hero is drawn to the Social Democrats. Yet when it comes to national destiny and a remedy for Germany's ills, it is not socialism that provides Cornelius with his answer. His ideology is based on a belief in the mystic relationship between man and his soil, on the conviction that like the giant of mythology men can

37

be restored to health and vigour through contact with the earth. The economic equivalent is a race of independent farmers tilling their hereditary land. The neglect of the small land-owner and the industrial explosion in the last three decades of the nineteenth century destroyed this relationship in Germany and accounts for the malaise of modern society. The nation is overpopulated and overcrowded. Its young men are forced to emigrate to alien lands and foreign colonies in search of fresh air and opportunity. Adventurous souls, we are told, become criminals because there is no proper outlet for their energies. One out of every three girls remains unmarried, her life blighted. These haphazard and contradictory reflections fall into place when Cornelius comes across a book on the colonial question written by a socialist, Hildebrand. It postulates the primacy of the productive agricultural class over the proletariat and industrial production. It advocates that private ownership of land be upheld and defended. No country, it argues, can afford a population greater than it can feed from its own resources. Since Germany is patently incapable of sustaining its population, it must expand into colonial territories. This simple argument is hammered home repeatedly by Cornelius and other characters and finally by Hans Grimm *in propria persona*.

What the novel therefore propagates is in effect a non-Marxist alternative to the problems of late capitalism, an alternative far more concrete and particular (but also more regressive) than Jünger's typological *Arbeiter* and his concept of total mobilization. Grimm seeks to deliver his compatriots from *Lohnknechtschaft*, from being enslaved by the wage-packet, from alienation, overcrowded slums and wasted lives. His solution is not class conflict and violent revolution but a national expansion which will bring reconciliation of conflicts and freedom from aggression within, while at the same time revolutionizing the quality of national life. (It was an argument rooted in the *völkisch* writings of Lagarde and Langbehn.) Where Jünger took the logic of economic rationalization and technological determinism to its ultimate conclusion, Grimm offers nothing more original than a recourse to *petit bourgeois* values. For all his indictment of capitalist evils, what he urges is a return to an earlier stage of economic history, to the age of the small-scale entrepreneur or peasant farmer with his alleged individualism, his independence, his readiness to seize opportunities and his cult of *Leistung* or achievement. In sociological terms the theory envisages not the restoration of the traditional *Bürgertum* but the enthronement of the lower middle class. Here surely is one of the reasons for the novel's enormous popularity under a regime which was carried to power on the fears and grievances of the *petite bourgeoisie*. Indeed the book contains various echoes of the original Nazi programme for social and economic reform.[23]

Grimm's perverse reasoning whereby an economic phenomenon is interpreted in geo-political terms is merely a symptom of the disease it ostensibly sets out to cure. Moreover, it is accompanied by indications of a biological racialism. Clearly these are endemic in the literature of European imperialism. The point is that Grimm's novel appeared not on the flood-tide of colonial expansion before 1914—during the author's formative period—but eight years *after* the War. In the light of the practical impossibility of then regaining a foothold in Africa, the book must inevitably have been read in relation to Nazi ideas of winning 'living space' in the eastern lands of Europe. Indeed it is now clear that Alfred Rosenberg in his *Mythus des Zwanzigsten Jahrhunderts* drew on Grimm's novel in arguing his case.[24] Rosenberg, the nearest to an ideologue that the NSDAP produced, demanded living space in much the same terms as Grimm. He too quoted declining population statistics in Germany. He too made the automatic connection between inner freedom and *Lebensraum*. The treatment of the plight of the peasants and of the industrial wilderness, the image of the Germanic character and achievements, the colonialist racialism are common to both. Rosenberg, like Grimm, distinguished between the trading English and the Germanic English; like Grimm too he condemned the *Entente* for leading native levies against their fellow white settlers. But Rosenberg in an attempt to win British support looked quite openly to Eastern Europe as providing the opportunity for fresh expansion and colonization.

Although nationalist resentment at the terms of the Versailles Treaty manifestly stimulated the popularity of Grimm's novel, it possessed other qualities calculated to appeal to a lower middle-class readership. Its enormous length stems from an endless accumulation of incident which combines a primitive desire for story-telling with a complete dearth of emotional or intellectual demands. Much of it is, in the words of one critic, 'an adventure story in the style of Karl May'[25] on whom several generations of German adolescents have fed their heroic fantasies. Grimm's hero remains static, an honest, diligent, fair-minded and ingenuous German Michel, who neither changes nor develops his personality but merely finds confirmation of his existing ideas. He embodies all those qualities such as simplicity, earnestness and fidelity which have traditionally been associated with the word *deutsch* since the eighteenth century. It is of course a prerequisite of crudely didactic writing of this kind, whatever the ideology behind it, that the dimension of critical distance be abolished and with it all intentional irony. The novel is written in an archaicizing, semi-literate style where the accumulation of emotive adjectives and a pseudo-Biblical syntax lend a spurious authority to the statements. *Volk ohne Raum* is generically a debased *Bildungsroman*, a novel of 'education and initiation', in which the vitality and moral insight of the original tradition have been swamped by sentimentality and pontification.

In the case of Grimm, as with so many contemporary intellectuals, we are reminded of Hegel's aphorism:

> An diesem, woran dem Geiste genügt, ist die Grösse seines Verlustes zu ermessen.
> (*The poverty of what now serves to satisfy the spirit is a measure of how much it has lost.*)

2. Ernst von Salomon: *Die Geächteten* (1931)

Grimm's bourgeois nature, his attachment to property, his uncomprehending attitude towards technology, his sentimentality, and his hostility towards the Soviet Union marked him off from the more radical and violent national revolutionaries. This younger generation of nationalists found a spokesman in Ernst von Salomon, as their French contemporaries turned to Drieu la Rochelle. His best-known work *Die Geächteten* is part autobiography, part reportage, part (though not overtly) fiction. It is a personal account of the *Freikorps* campaigns in the period immediately after the First World War and of the political conspiracies which led to the assassination of Walther Rathenau. Its interest lies less in the military or political facts of these campaigns than in Von Salomon's interpretation of events. The ideological framework of the book is familiar from studies of the 'conservative revolution'. What is unique is the experience of a lived ethos which no abstract analysis can produce. In its own perverse way it is a far more impressive achievement than Johst's *Schlageter* which deals with a similar theme. In the narrator's opening account of the chaotic days of November 1918 two features emerge which prove characteristic of the rest of the book: the primacy of idealistic values over material factors and the insidious use of highly charged emotional language which anticipates (or mirrors) the concepts of an ideology. The narrator displays a now familiar unwillingness or inability to entertain a rational political debate or analysis. He is not prepared to acknowledge the political will of the masses or any objective justification for their rebellion. Instead of a working population driven to desperation by four years of war, virtual famine and repression, he sees only a mob epitomizing the red peril of Bismarckian days.

In the men who enlist for frontier defence in the East, the desire for self-liberation and fulfilment is ultimately more significant than patriotic pride. The campaigns in the East offer a chance to compensate for the unacknowledged defeat in the West. These volunteers live for the intensity of combat and are dedicated to the cult of action. They feel a constantly repeated need to prove themselves in the face of danger and hardship, to demand of themselves the utmost in courage, strength and endurance. The narrator vividly describes the intoxication of battle, the delirious excitement, the mindless impetus, the blood lust which demands consummation, the almost erotic elation that he experiences in the fusion of man, weapon and victim. The mystique of violence is invoked no less powerfully than the mystique of *Blut und Boden,* of the rich soil which was once fertilized by the blood of earlier German conquerors and which the *Freikorps* are now pledged to defend. The narrator's ambivalence towards the Bolsheviks, the mixture of hatred and respect that he displays, anticipates the National Bolshevism of Ernst Niekisch.[26] The common enemy of both the Bolsheviks and the German patriots is the capitalist West. The narrator comes to feel that in the Baltic he and his comrades have allowed themselves to be used as the instruments of sordid political scheming. If the *Freikorps* had already made one fatal blunder in helping to restore law and order in Germany in 1918–19, they have now committed a second error in permitting themselves to be used as mercenaries of the *Entente* against the Red Army and against a nation which, like the Germans themselves, is struggling to achieve its freedom.

In *Die Geächteten* political discussions are dominated by the powerful clichés of unreason. Politics for their opponents is a matter of self-interest, a means of satisfying material needs. For the narrator and his comrades, however, it is a question of obeying a metaphysical law and partaking of a deeper reality. The notion of Fate or Destiny is frequently invoked as the ultimate arbiter of human events or as the justification for political action. The *Freikorps* feel they have a mission to mould the as yet inchoate Reich (a millennial fiction not to be confused with actual political boundaries) according to their will, their vision. For

41

this they are prepared to sacrifice not only their lives but even their conscience and their integrity. Ultimately the conflict in which they are involved is hypostasized into a struggle between God and the Devil, with themselves as a doomed elect, a generation of provisionals. Thus their position is unassailable by reason. Convinced that they are the chosen, they interpet even practical failure as temporary, for History is on their side. And the strength of their faith itself betokens its validity. The value of a belief is measured not in any objective terms but by the degree of personal commitment it commands. For the time being they are content with intuitive apprehension or the instinctive response of the blood. The reward for perseverance and steadfastness will be full revelation and knowledge. The ends are so absolute as to justify the most squalid political means: murder, robbery, sabotage, torture. Various aspects of the Idealist tradition are brought together here in their ultimate, catastrophically travestied form. The inwardness and other-worldliness, now so terribly at odds with political realities, issue inevitably in death. In the glorification of death as a return to the womb of Nature this political romanticism achieves its appropriate culmination.

The assassination of Rathenau in 1922 marks the climax of the terrorist campaigns of the *Freikorps* men after they have been driven underground. Rathenau, Foreign Minister and living symbol of the Weimar Republic, must die because he threatens to restore Germany's self-confidence and to persuade the people to live according to his values which to the radicals are those of a fossilized corrupt world, in other words lukewarm patriotism, bourgeois materialism, servility and a sentimental cosmopolitanism. The narrator is subsequently sickened by the failure of Rathenau's death to bring about any change in the seamy, cliché-ridden world of German politics.

Von Salomon's book may not be always a strictly accurate record. There are certain minor inconsistencies between *Die Geächteten* and the autobiography and apologia he published in 1951 entitled *Der Fragebogen*. Moreover the account of his own exploits in the Baltic campaigns begins to strain our credulity somewhat when we realize that he was still a boy of seventeen with no wartime experience behind him. He casts himself in a mould that strongly suggests adolescent wish-fulfilment. Yet this matters little if one considers the undoubted fidelity with which he articulates the feelings and aspirations of his social group, the young intellectuals who flocked to the conservative anti-democratic movements of the Weimar Republic. These student idealists who together with uprooted and disinherited war veterans made up the majority of *Freikorps* recruits, helped to encourage hostility towards the Republic and to foster the cult of violence.[27] But in 1933 the hour of reckoning came for Von Salomon no less than for Ernst Jünger and Gottfried Benn. The archival material entrusted to him by his old *Freikorps* comrades was hastily presented to the national archives lest it should be confiscated by the Gestapo or the Party, and he himself eked out a comfortable if inglorious existence until the end of the War as a film-script writer with Ufa, the state-controlled film studio.

Chapter Three
The Literature of Constatation

Neue Sachlichkeit

If the Expressionist mode corresponded to the turbulence of the War and its immediate aftermath, the kind of writing known as *Neue Sachlichkeit* belonged properly to the years when the Weimar Republic achieved a brief and illusory stability. The term itself was coined in 1925 when G. F. Hartlaub used it in the title of an exhibition of neo-realistic painting at Mannheim. After the pathos and emphatic rhetoric, the utopianism or the bizarre nightmares of the Expressionist years came a period of disenchantment and reassessment. The 'objectivism'[1] of writers such as Erich Kästner, Hermann Kesten or Joseph Roth sprang from a determined acceptance of contemporary social conditions. It involved a laconic attempt to reflect the reality of the day. Inevitably, however, in the context of the time, this was tantamount to committing oneself to 'Western' values. With their ironic scepticism, their fascination with urban and industrial life, their journalistic idiom and their terse functionality, the objectivists appeared profoundly un-German to the right wing and to those 'apolitical' intellectuals who were already plunging into mythopoeic irrationalism. Under the pressures of Weimar the very choice of subject and its treatment involved—perhaps unwittingly—an ideological decision, no matter how non-committal the overt position of the writer. As the economic and political crisis came to a head at the turn of the decade, most objectivist writers found themselves left of centre. Some became Marxists and joined the KPD. The majority formed a nucleus of what was called a 'white socialism', an attitude that was increasingly critical of capitalism and impatient with the failure of liberal democracy. They even adopted a Marxist terminology, although without necessarily accepting its basis in dialectical materialism. Up to the end of the decade *Neue Sachlichkeit* was the literary home of an ideologically homeless left.

As Lukács pointed out in his attack on Ernst Ottwalt,[2] the initial one-sided stress on content had nevertheless led to a degree of formal experiment. For in order to be true to modern experience, to reproduce it in an adequate manner, the objectivist writers had to seek new techniques. Their most characteristic literary innovation was the documentary form. The documentary in this sense sprang from the desire to authenticate a literary statement about contemporary life or the recent past by overt reference to verifiable historical data. It differed from the traditional use of historical documents in literature in several ways. First, it was concerned to make a relevant statement about current issues, not about a remote historical situation. Secondly, it was not interested in setting off individual characters against a recognizable background but rather in conveying the texture and flavour of a contemporary social milieu. The emphasis lay on circumstances rather than on personalities. Thirdly, the use of documents or authentic sources was built into the work itself, either in the form of a preface and appendices or as an integral part of the text. Documentary literature moves away from traditional realist *Gestaltung* towards montage and reportage. The writer sees himself as an editor rather than an inventor or creator, though there can be wide and crucial divergences in the extent to which his material is selected, shaped, structured, refined and adapted.

An early German example of the genre, anticipating the objectivist use of the documentary by several years, is Karl Kraus' anti-war drama *Die letzten Tage der Menschheit*, the earliest scenes of which date from 1917. In his preface Kraus claimed that he had done little more than body forth speeches, dialogues and printed documents. In fact, however, Kraus had not merely edited his material or amassed a series of quotations. He had also stylized and recreated it in dramatic form. Though the dialogue is brilliantly realistic in its use of slang, colloquialisms and professional jargon, and though many situations are authenticated, the particular speeches and characters are for the most part invented. Though there is no conventional dramatic plot or protagonist, the play is given a dramatic unity and a structured development through the use of recurring motifs, repetition, contrast and balance. In the last act Kraus' imagination reaches mythic proportions. Cinematic sequences are combined with grotesque Expressionist fantasies, ending in the Apocalypse. His successors a decade later imitated the documentary approach but self-consciously kept their imagination in check. Thus Ernst Ottwalt notes at the beginning of a novel exposing the prejudices, chicanery and corruption of the German judiciary, that he is prepared to answer any queries from his readers as to the factual basis of his accusations. Theodor Plivier's 'novel of the German Fleet',[3] which records a group experience and abounds in technical descriptions

45

of running and maintaining a ship, introduces in its final section a first-person narrator to assure the reader, somewhat lamely, of its authenticity. Ernst Toller tackled his documentary drama *Feuer aus den Kesseln* (1930) more methodically, reproducing in a lengthy appendix the sources upon which he had drawn. But he also changed locations and chronology in the interests of dramatic concentration or effectiveness and felt free to invent new characters.[4] He reserved his right to distinguish between creative art and mere reportage, while agreeing that on matters of substance artistic statements must be congruent with historical truth. In fact it is clear that Toller adapted his material just as much in the interests of a political message as in those of artistic form. Toller's play reveals a move away from his earlier, more dialectic drama towards direct agitatory impact. His play was not only a tribute to revolutionary action but also an indictment of the political justice of 1930. The prosecutors and judges of 1917 were still members of the judiciary and Toller publicly challenged them to answer his charges. For a final example of the documentary genre one might look at Erik Reger's novel *Union der festen Hand* where he drew on his first-hand experience of working for Krupp and barely disguised the historical models for his exposure of German industry (Krupp, Stinnes, Thyssen, Hugenberg and others). They are given fictitious names only to raise them to a representative level.[5]

Documentary writing had an obvious appeal in the age of the film camera and the radio microphone. Nowadays much of it has only a documentary interest. Its only aesthetic (as distinct from didactic) justification is surely the means it offers of articulating a reality whose horrendous perversity seems to surpass and paralyse the literary imagination. There are a small number of examples (Kraus' play is one, Weiss' *Die Ermittlung* another) which, in the very act of confessing their inability to devise an adequate aesthetic equivalent for a reality that defies the imagination, reassert their creative power and transcend their dilemma. Only through a documentary approach can they avoid 'aestheticizing'—in other words, betraying and attenuating—the experiences which furnish their terrible subject matter. Yet that kind of 'documentary' is no mere accumulation of *faits divers* where bareness threatens to become barrenness. It is still informed by meaningful patterns or by a search for the overall meaning of events.[6] The discreet artistic shaping is synonymous with an existential interpretation—socio-economic in the one case, apocalyptic in the other. The documentary writing of objectivism, however, is not of that order.

The World of Weimar

In a world in which the laws of the market place dominated even literary life, two best-sellers conveyed a sense of the alienation and despairing passivity that were so widespread among the non-aligned Weimar intellectuals. Erich Kästner's novel *Fabian* (1931) is probably the closest German equivalent to the Berlin stories of Christopher Isherwood. It traces the adventures of the ingenuous hero through the Berlin of the Depression, when republican democracy had already ceded to authoritarianism and the extremists on either side were vying with one another for the final victory. Fabian stands in the centre of the ideological storm. His only defence against society is a rather flippant wit and a battered but still basically sound sense of personal integrity. Clad in this inadequate armour he drifts through the frenzied, chaotic life of the city, unable to discern any purpose or meaning in existence, helpless to influence or challenge his milieu. Nightmare visions embody his experience of social alienation and the vicious, predatory nature of advanced capitalism. And whenever Fabian considers the political scene his wry *aperçus* convey his pessimism and resignation. Beneath his ironic, self-deprecating charm Fabian suffers not only from his personal inadequacies but also from the pestilence of the age in which he lives. His scruples, his mistrust of power and his sceptical insight into his contemporaries' motives prevent him from seeking a remedy in any given political cause. But his resignation is painful and his isolation hard to endure.

Hans Fallada confined his novel *Kleiner Mann—was nun?* (1932) to a worm's eye view of the lower middle-class victims of the Depression. The protagonist, Pinneberg, struggles to defend his private happiness against the encroachments of the economic crisis. His intermediate position between the established middle class on the one hand, and a proletariat he despises on the other, proves in the long run untenable. In his gnawing insecurity, his ever present fear of redundancy, Pinneberg realizes that the grey masses of the proletariat are the only conceivable comrades for him. Yet he dreads being reduced to their social level and having to abandon his hard-won status, however little it avails him. The historical consequences of his predicament are not drawn: instead of voting for fascism like his contemporaries, he finds solace in a sentimental domestic idyll. Likewise Fallada offers no objective analysis of the economic crisis. His hero appears to be at the mercy of anonymous, threatening forces, the plaything of a malevolent fate. He is thus effectively absolved of personal responsibility, while his helpless passivity amounts to an affirmation of events. The novel faithfully mirrors the plight of the *petite bourgeoisie* instead of providing a critique of it.

Ernst Toller's play *Hoppla, wir leben!* (1927), a work which takes us into the heart of Weimar political life, was the product of close co-operation with Erwin Piscator and shows his influence on the technical side of its production with its use of film, loudspeakers and a 'construc-tivist' set.[7] Using a traditional device of *Verfremdung* Toller examines his own society through the eyes of a stranger, a former revolutionary recently released from a mental hospital to which his traumatic experi-ences in 1919 had condemned him. Karl Thomas is a *revenant* who reminds his former comrades of the ideals for which they once fought and faced death. And his naïve bemusement at their new-found prag-matism is a measure of the debasement of those ideals at the 'dirty hands' of politics.[8] The hero realizes that the one great event of his life, the only thing that gives meaning to his existence and sustains him against the threat of despair, has become a mere episode in the eyes of others, to be glossed over in silence or forgotten under the pressure of new events and fresh challenges. His final speech transcends the political scene and opens up a vista of metaphysical absurdity. Yet that vision is Karl's and his alone: it is not the final statement of the play. At the very moment of Karl's suicide the dramatist provides a pointed reminder of the social evils which remain to be combated, and the value of comradeship is affirmed anew by the reactions of Karl's friends in the adjoining cells. We are left with a feeling of chagrin that a man of impassioned humane idealism should find no place in this society. But we are also left with the assurance that his comrades will persevere in the fight to make the world a more tolerable place to live in.

1. Erik Reger: *Union der festen Hand* (1931)

Hitherto I have briefly mentioned works which reproduce the texture of Weimar life. A more probing, analytical treatment is to be found in Reger's *Union der festen Hand*. The subtitle of the novel reads 'Roman einer Entwicklung' (the story of an evolution). The allusion to the *Bildungsroman* tradition seems deliberate. It arouses expectations of a tale of moral, intellectual and emotional development from youth to maturity. Just as deliberately the book soon explodes those expectations, for the novel belongs unmistakably to the twentieth century. Its foreground deals not with the development of a single individual but with the economic and social history of Weimar Germany, with a period when personality is defined in terms of social function and occupation rather than in terms of intrinsic human qualities. By implicitly drawing our attention in this way to the reinterpretation of the fictional task, Reger arouses our critical alertness. It is a minor example of a technique applied throughout the book: the distancing of the reader from the personal histories narrated and the maintaining of a critical detachment vis-à-vis social and economic developments. Reger's novel is an attempt to 'alienate' the reader from his environment in the Brechtian sense of making the familiar appear unfamiliar. And where Brecht drew on various technical resources of the theatre or modified the structure of his dramas to achieve *Verfremdung*, Reger evolves methods more appropriate to the narrative mode. The results are not perhaps as rich or as diverse as in the case of the 'epic' theatre. Yet they prove highly effective in the context of this unjustly neglected novel.

Reger divides the book into five sections whose titles chart the successive stages in the history of industrial power from the end of the War. And at the close of each section he introduces a newspaper report which sums up the main developments in the preceding period or complements these by reference to events elsewhere in Germany. These reports also serve to set the scene for the next section. The contrasting reportage style interrupts the flow of the narrative and encourages a pause for reflection not only on the events themselves but also on the way they are reported in the press. The reader is urged to study the functioning of the mechanisms exposed here, so that after the fifth section he will be able to write his own newspaper summary. This appeal to critical reflection is reinforced by another device. At intervals political slogans and clichés are printed in upper case, without comment, in a context which reveals only too clearly the disparity between what they ostensibly denote and the reality in which they are glibly invoked. Reger also recognized the importance of the narrator as a foil to the flow of events. His narrative voice, unlike Fallada's, is not content merely to record the surface of events from a private perspective: it explains, analyses, demonstrates, makes significant connections and retains a rational insight into the milieu it describes even when the milieu is raised to an irrational power. On the other hand, faced with the outcome, the narrator cannot offer any simple remedy.

The major achievement of Reger's novel is to have exposed the process of economic rationalization in Germany after the War and to have traced the manner in which heavy industry preserved, entrenched and expanded its power under the Republic. When we meet a representative group of industrialists at the end of the War, it soon becomes clear that Reger intends to go far beyond the caricatures of party propaganda. His concern is to differentiate between the various generations of industrial chiefs to show the development of the capitalist system itself, from the self-made entrepreneurs of the *Gründerjahre* (the first phase of industrial expansion after the unification of Germany), to the commercial adventurers of a later phase, the industrial bureaucrats, and finally the *Händler*, the faceless financiers of the 1920s.[9]

In this final stage we hear of massive exchanges of shares, complex deals, intricate partnership arrangements, numerous take-overs and instances of asset-stripping, manoeuvres so involved and obscure that the public cannot keep track of events. In the name of rationalization Hillgruber, the archetypal *Händler*, instigates the formation of a trust, a monolithic monster that devours all competitors. Only a few meaningless balance sheets reach the outside world. Shareholders are powerless to control the company directors. Workers no longer know who really employs them and lose interest in the destination of the things they produce. Hillgruber in short introduces a totalitarian phase in industrial history. Moreover, it is equally clear that these cartels, syndicates and trusts dominate and threaten to devour even their creators. The human mind can no longer keep pace with its own monstrous progeny.

The emergence of this ultimate stage in the development of capitalism cannot be separated from the history of relations between industry and government. The relationship is governed by weakness and miscalculation on the one hand and by unscrupulous self-aggrandizement on the other. The government looks on helplessly as the process of rationalization gathers momentum, for it is now evident that industry and finance rule the state, not the politicians and least of all the electorate. Intimidated by the spectre of unemployment, cabinets hasten to equate the profits of heavy industry with the national good. When rationalization fails in the long run to produce the expected economic miracle, when the consequences of colossal mismanagement make themselves felt, the industrialists turn the Weimar Republic into a scapegoat for their own blunders. They make its social policies responsible for the sickness of the economy. With seductive logic, with a masterly balance of lucid exposition and rhetorical appeal, a combination of emotional, idealistic and materialistic formulations, the industrialists argue that the German workers are pricing themselves out of the world markets. They claim that the true enemies and exploiters of the working class are not the employers but the politicians and bureaucrats who put their self-interest and careers above all else. With this assault on the republican hands that have fed them, the industrialists begin to campaign for the removal of all the safeguards and agreements won by the trade unions since the War. Lay-offs, redundancies and lock-outs further wear down the resistance of the workers. Meanwhile, behind the scenes the industrialists have established contacts with the Nazis, as part of their plan to smash the residual power of the unions. They regard the Nazi ideology as insane but concede that the Party has a useful function to perform in bringing pressure to bear on other social groups and on foreign opinion. The 'Union der festen Hand', as the industrialists' alliance is known, considers the Nazis to be completely under its control. The Nazis for their part are eager to be all things to all men, an opportunism facilitated by the vagueness and confusion of their slogans.

Reger's novel is not only a highly perspicacious account of the growth of industrial power during the Weimar Republic. It is also a relentless exposure of the *débâcle* of working class militancy during these same years. Here we find no heroicization, no myth of the collective, no dogged determination, no tragic pathos. Reger's sometimes sardonic analysis of the self-seeking quietism of the average German worker goes a long way towards explaining why socialism failed and fascism triumphed during the lifetime of the Republic. The workers believe they have far more to lose than their chains: there is the discount store, the doctor, the maternity home, the social club and the company pension. The political implications of *embourgeoisement* become clear. The workers would exchange all their hard-won rights and concessions for a few extra pfennigs an hour. One of the employers reflects on the desperate desire of many workers to see themselves or their children graduate into the ranks of the bourgeoisie. Their models, their goals, their mental attitudes are governed by bourgeois precedents. The fourth estate, he concludes, is no more than a degraded middle class bent on rehabilitating itself. Even when, as in 1918–19, the workers have a measure of power, they fritter it away for want of effective leadership and a clear political purpose. During the Weimar years they grow successively more demoralized and indifferent. Radical gestures give way to bureaucratic protest. The legacy of political authoritarianism has left them steeped in a quasi-military discipline: if their songs have socialist texts, the melodies are old army tunes. And as times become

51

harder the workers prove susceptible to the appeals of the *Stahlhelm* (the militant, right-wing ex-servicemen's organization), and the Nazis. Finally, a free newspaper, expensively and skilfully edited, is launched to overcome the workers' sense of alienation, to instil management values and reconcile them to their lot.

The character through whose experience we witness much of this demoralization and decline is Adam Griguszies, who begins as an arrogantly stupid Communist agitator but ends by uttering the last hopeless lines of the novel:

Was bedeuten sie?	*(What do they represent?*
Veteranen der Arbeit?	*Horny-handed sons of toil?*
Opfer des Kapitals?	*Victims of capitalism?*
Erwachendes Deutschland?	*Germany awakening?*
Soldaten der Roten Armee?	*Soldiers of the Red Army?*
Du lieber Gott. Du lieber	*Dear God in Heaven . . . Dear God*
Gott.—	*in Heaven . . .)*

The present-day reader is well placed to supply that final newspaper report which Reger withheld so as not to anticipate the course of events.

2. Thomas Mann: *Mario und der Zauberer* (1930)

In his epic novel *Der Zauberberg* Thomas Mann escorted his young hero through a series of ideological and existential temptations to an epiphany of love and hope. Hans Castorp was the symbol of a Germany faced with a choice between Western values and its own Romantic heritage, between a dark irrationalism pregnant with disaster and new, life-enhancing patterns of thought and feeling. In the novel the hero glimpses where the choice should lie—in mediating between and transcending the opposites—without having the strength of conviction and moral will to commit himself to it. And the depiction of his tempters and mentors is likewise hedged about with ironic ambiguity. But if this aesthetic statement is complex and qualified, with a conclusion which posits no solution within the novel but appeals to the historical responsibility of the reader to shape his own answers in the social world outside the book, Mann's publicistic support for the Republic after 1922 grew increasingly forthright. He was one of several leading German intellectuals (among them Ernst Troeltsch, Friedrich Meinecke and Walther Rathenau) who moved from a conservative, authoritarian position to one of realistic acceptance of the post-war state, thereby earning for themselves the title of *Vernunftrepublikaner*.[10] Though intellectually convinced of the need for a Republic, they weakened their standing and their cause by being less than passionately committed to its support, particularly in the early years. Mann's own initial statements contained a good deal of shameless casuistry. However, his special contribution was to elucidate the perils of the non-political tradition of which he had once been such a determined advocate, and to emphasize the dangers of a misguided idealism.[11] He defined the greatest temptation of the modern intelligentsia as the desire to slough off the principle of individuation, to regress to mythic, unconscious depths, to return to the instinctive springs of being. It thus became susceptible to political totalitarianism. Mann was under no illusion as to the facile optimism and shallow positivism of so much 'democratic' thinking. But he felt that under the circumstances the Republic offered the best—indeed, the only—chance of defending the moral and cultural values which he subsumed under the notion of *Humanität*. Shortly after the crucial elections of 1930 he appealed to the German bourgeoisie to support the Social Democrats in future polls in order to check the rise of fascism.

If that same public had read his latest story *Mario und der Zauberer*, it might understandably have questioned the connection between his political rhetoric and this tale of an Italian hypnotist. The point is that Mann's *novella* transposes into the setting of a seaside entertainment the author's ideas on the nature of political leadership in a fascist dictatorship.[12] Furthermore it hints at private doubts and reservations which election speeches could only mask, never suppress. Not once is it stated that this apparently simple tale of a hypnotist shot dead by one of his subjects is a political parable. However, a series of internal references and allusions suggest parallels with the fascist Italy in which the story takes place. From the outset the narrator establishes the chauvinism of the Italian bourgeoisie, its servility, authoritarian injustice and self-conscious puritanism. Cipolla's own asides to the audience express a self-assertive nationalism. His commentary repeatedly points to the problem of political power and leadership and at one stage he even gives Mario the fascist salute in honour of the heroic tradition of the Fatherland.

Cipolla is physically repugnant, an asthmatic hunchback with bad or broken teeth. His bitter malice towards the strong, the healthy and the virile hints at the compensatory function which his highly developed will-power fulfils. He is full of contempt for his victims and relishes their humiliation. His voice proves stronger than reason, virtue, duty, pride or love—cynically belying, in fact, all the qualities which as a patriot he is pledged to uphold. It seems that his victims succumb to the negativity of their position. They simply try to resist Cipolla's will without being very clear or convinced about what it is they champion. Their liberty has become an abstraction, an end in itself, rather than a truly positive value linked to the achievement of definable goals. The story thus suggests that the audience's susceptibility is due, at least in part, to a disjunction between the ethos it wishes to uphold and the social or political forms in which those values ought to be cast—an inconsequentiality rooted in a loss of faith which Cipolla knows full well how to exploit.[13] Cipolla's will to power is by contrast concerted and dynamic. Yet to sustain it calls for a constant, unflagging effort, with frequent recourse to stimulants to revive his stamina. Thus he presents himself as the suffering, self-sacrificing leader and even appeals to his audience's compassion, assuring them that to command is synonymous with obeying.

But Cipolla is not only a clever hypnotist, he is also a master of rhetoric. And the welter of paradox and mystification with which he surrounds his act is only too familiar from justifications of the *Volksdiktatur*, whereby the leader's will to power is sanctioned as the voice of the people. There can be little doubt as to who is the master in that sultry seaside hall. Yet Cipolla's words suggest a dependence which is not entirely fictitious. Though not in the way he describes, there is indeed a mutual bond between him and his audience, for he needs them as the objects of his will. In fact he is even emotionally dependent upon them. This is no detached, superior master-mind but a lonely, deformed, all-too-human figure who can only make contact with his fellow men by dominating them. The will to power in Cipolla represents a perversion of the desire to be loved, as can be seen from the transvestite substitution in which his act culminates. And it is precisely at this point that Cipolla's concentration falters. By allowing his dependence to come to the fore, Cipolla weakens the willpower into which it has been channelled. His hold over the young waiter Mario slackens and allows the hapless victim to awaken to a dazed realization of the humiliation inflicted upon him. Mario is the only victim who remembers what has happened in the hypnotic trance—because Cipolla's will was not strong enough to erase the memory. Cipolla is not destroyed by any external agency or force triumphantly pitted against him—paradoxically, Mario is a far more ineffectual figure than many of the previous victims —but by his own weakness, his own loss of self-control.

Whom did Mann have in mind, if anybody? The obvious example of physical deficiency in the Nazi hierarchy was Goebbels, with his club foot and hypertrophic intellect. It was Brecht who, in *Der aufhaltsame Aufstieg des Arturo Ui*, obliquely suggested this connection by calling his own caricature of Goebbels 'Givolla'. Goebbels, the intellectual apostate, may well have been more interesting to Mann than Hitler's semi-literate banality. But then Cipolla's whip also recalls Streicher, while the perversity of his sexual constitution contains an echo of Röhm's notorious homosexuality.

What of Mann's narrator who witnesses and recalls these events, who provides us with a critical view of the performance and seems to possess a more lucid insight into Cipolla's behaviour than anyone else present? The narrator is in fact a distinct personality, not merely an anonymous voice. And before long he gives us the impression of being on the defensive, as though he were anticipating objections which he is anxious to discount. It emerges that despite his moral misgivings the narrator is clearly fascinated by Cipolla's act and is prevented from leaving or interrupting the performance by his desire for further revelations and instructive experiences, however pernicious or uncanny they may prove (a mark of the 'true' moralist, according to Mann's *Betrachtungen eines Unpolitischen*). The real source of his uneasiness and guilt is not the neglect of his parental duty. It is the tacit recognition that he has become Cipolla's accomplice. His sin of omission has helped to bring about a catastrophe which his intelligence and moral insight might have prevented. The narrator may present himself as a detached, objective observer but in reality he is as much in thrall to Cipolla as anyone else present. The degradation suffered by the individual victims dishonours the whole audience, as the narrator himself tells us. But whereas the others are unsuspecting and gullible, oblivious to the full implications of what is going on, the narrator by virtue of his insight and acquiescence is *guilty*. We may perhaps conclude that his fascination is aesthetic in origin: he recognizes and admires in Cipolla a masterly performer, an artist in language, a 'brother in the spirit'.[14]

It would be egregious to identify Mann with the narrator. The latter gives himself away precisely because of the ironic distance between the novelist and his character. Yet irony is itself an aesthetic, not a moral quality. We do well to bear in mind Mann's admission when he justified his abandonment of the conservative position:

> Ich habe vielleicht meine Gedanken geändert—nicht meinen Sinn.[15]
> (*I may have changed my opinions—but not my drift.*)

Chapter Four
The Literature of the Third Reich

A. Nazi Writing[1]

When Hitler came to power the racial and political purge of national institutions proceeded apace. Every aspect of cultural activity was rapidly integrated into a tightly organized system of direction and control. The majority of democratic or socialist writers went into exile. Those who stayed, either by design or because they failed to escape in time, ended in prison or in the camps. The reconstituted Prussian Academy of Arts included among its new members Hans Carossa, Hans Grimm, Gustav Frenssen and Guido Kolbenheyer. The *Sektion für Dichtkunst* wanted to elect Stefan George as president in place of Heinrich Mann but since George had emigrated to Switzerland in spite of Goebbels' inducements, they had to settle for the erstwhile Expressionist playwright Hanns Johst. Three separate censorship authorities controlled literary production. Overnight the sole criterion of literary merit became ideological correctness, while literary criticism was reduced to a matter of eulogy or defamation. By 1936 analytical criticism and evaluation were formally abolished by Goebbels in favour of a purely interpretative *Kunstbericht* which would simply pay tribute to and describe a work of art.[2] Goebbels' directive to the German theatre on 9 May 1933, laying down the guidelines for the official aesthetic, contained a typical self-contradiction, but also an unambiguous threat:

> Die deutsche Kunst der nächsten Jahrzehnte wird heroisch, wird stählern, romantisch, wird sentimentalitätslos sachlich, wird national mit grossem Pathos, sie wird gemeinsam, verpflichtend und bindend sein oder sie wird nicht sein.[3]
> (*German art in the coming decades will be heroic, steely, romantic, it will be unsentimental and down to earth, patriotic with great fervour, it will be communal, committed and binding or else it will cease to exist.*)

The aims of such a literature were to preserve the *Volk* and the State

56

from dangerous influences, to be an instrument of political education and to bear witness to National Socialist achievements.

One of the main characteristics of Nazi literature, then, was its anti-intellectualism. For reason and critical analysis, it substituted instinct, intuition, unquestioning faith and the bonds of racial unity. It condemned the Enlightenment spirit as un-German, shallow, decadent and destructive, and instead glorified the German 'heart' or 'soul' with its associations of inwardness and metaphysical profundity. But it also repudiated the complexities and ambiguities of aesthetic modernism in favour of a much-vaunted clarity, simplicity and directness. Nazi writers set out to invent a new mythology based primarily on a free interpretation of the heroic Nordic past. They identified *deutsch* with *germanisch* and cultivated a barbaric paganism to which even Christianity was subordinated. Together with the party ideologues they provided the political take-over with a pseudo-philosophical superstructure. A Darwinistic view of society and history, notions of biological selection and mutation, helped to justify the regime's right to rule. The will to power was affirmed as the driving spring of human creativity. At the same time the blood of the race was propounded as the mythic ground of being, providing both internal cohesion and an exclusive homogeneity in the face of influences or assaults from outside. The *Volksgemeinschaft*, the racial community, harmonious and united, was contrasted with an atomistic, mechanistic *Gesellschaft*, riven by strife and constantly threatened by anarchy.

The literature of National Socialism invoked a historical fatalism in its ideological struggle against doubt and scruple. Fate was the ultimate controlling power in human affairs, mysterious, unfathomable, absolute in its compulsion—and the test of heroism was the instinctive commitment to Fate's decrees, the 'decision' which produced action and deed with no thought for personal suffering or loss. The cult of heroism in this sense of pursuing one's destiny to the bitter end figured prominently in Nazi writing. The Führer was presented as the tool of history or Fate or some other transcendental force. His charismatic leadership was invested with a religious or mythic awe and personal fulfilment could be sought only in the execution of his will. As far as the outside world was concerned, however, the relationship between *Führer* and *Gefolge*, overlord and vassals, was transformed into the basis of a new imperialism, a justification of the natural right of the German people or the Aryan race to rule over subordinate or inferior nations. The virtues which were said to have laid the foundation of Germany's greatness were simplicity, honesty, obedience, loyalty and discipline. The life of the individual was dedicated to the service and glory of the *Volk*. The concept of a 'Prussian socialism' sought to fuse the patriotic militarist heritage with the anti-liberalism and anti-Marxism of the conservative middle class. These German values had to be preserved through racial hygiene and physical purity, through the cult of health and beauty. The *Volk* had to be constantly on its guard against possible polluters of the nation and other unwholesome influences.

Nowhere was the stress on racial purity and strength more prominent than in the *Heimatdichtung* and the formula of 'blood and soil'. The bond of blood, of heredity and heritage, was reinforced by a pseudo-mystic communion with the soil which had the property to purify and regenerate human nature. The formula was associated with a cult of elemental passions and fertility, of full-blooded manhood and the earth-mother. An anti-urban polemic which had once praised the qualities of health, uprightness, simplicity, *Gemüt* and a rough-hewn authenticity, now degenerated into primitivism, brutality and fanaticism. The German peasant farmer was mythologized no less than the front-line soldier: he became a timeless figure, strong, defiant, grave and brooding, his own ploughman, sower and reaper, master of his land and fate, more interested in ritual than artificial fertilizer.[4] Idealization and deliberate archaisms combined to produce an anti-historical genre which eschewed concrete economic or social problems in favour of ideological wish-fulfilment. Significantly, what we here find projected on to a rural setting are the dreams and fears of an *urban* lower middle class seeking to escape the consequences of its absorption into a modern, pluralist industrial society. Such 'novels of the soil' soon accounted for more than half the fiction titles recommended each year by the Party.

The motifs of the war experience and of the '*Volk ohne Raum*' complemented the mythic presentation of peasant life in the repertoire of Nazi literature. Other standard themes involved the glorification of the 'brown battalions', the Party militant, and the plight of the *Auslandsdeutschen* who dwelt amid hostile, jealous nations and yearned to be reunited with the fatherland. Yet the regime failed in two important aspects of its literary policy. It was unsuccessful in its efforts to manipulate for its own ends the vogue of historical fiction; and similarly, it failed to encourage the writing of novels devoted to contemporary social and political realities, the *Zeitroman*.

There was nothing revolutionary about the language of Nazi litera-

ture. Whether in prose or poetry, it was markedly epigonal.[5] Stefan
George was hailed as the father of the new lyric on the basis of *Das
Neue Reich* (1928) and a handful of other poems such as 'Krieg'. He
seemed to preach a new racial consciousness and the need for a strong
völkisch state and leader (though in fact his was a millennial vision
vouchsafed only to a spiritual and aesthetic elite). His heroic pathos was
readily imitated, as were his metaphors of flame and blood. But the
primitive eclecticism of the Nazi ideology was matched by the indis-
criminate exploitation of a variety of literary and linguistic sources. The
forms and rhythms owed much to the nationalist poetry of the Napole-
onic era and the 1840s. Wagner's alliterative Nibelung style also left
its traces. The vocabulary of '*Blut und Boden*' mingled with a Germanic
or medieval idiom. Religious terminology reinforced and sanctified the
Party's claim to power. The eulogizing of Hitler again deliberately
invoked religious, especially Messianic associations or reiterated hack-
neyed historical images. Nazi poetry was a public affair, the profession
of a creed, recited at social gatherings, festivals, or celebrations. Choral
songs of the collective alternated with liturgical *Fahnen-* or *Weihesprüche*
in which the individual pledged himself to serve the Party and the *Volk*
and appealed to others to follow his example. The high-minded idealism
of sacrifice and dedication accorded ill with outbursts of brutal aggression against the enemies of the people. Attempts at dramatic innovations—*Chorspiele*, cantatas, *Thingspiele*—looked suspiciously like
the mass theatre favoured by the Socialists in the days of the Republic;
at all events they failed to capture the imagination of even a well-disposed
audience.

In retrospect it seems as though the most important fascist literature
was written before 1933. Thereafter, for one reason and another, not
least because of the profound disparity between ideology and reality, it
appears to lose its impetus and inspiration. Many of the successful
works of the Nazi period were new editions or impressions of older
books. Authors of repute to whom the Nazis looked for support (above
all George, Jünger and Benn) refused to harness their imaginative
energies to the Party. By the late thirties only the ageing Gerhart
Hauptmann allowed the regime to benefit from his international
prestige. Consequently these years saw the flowering of a literary
mediocrity so banal and incompetent that even the Party leaders
themselves became concerned about the lack of creative talent. In
short, Nazi literature remained versified ideology produced by inferior
poetasters who, in the words of one critic, tried to stimulate their

readers with a meaningless torrent of emotive clichés designed to have an indeterminate irritant effect.[6]

Modernism was linked in the Nazi mind with biological decadence, Jewish perfidy and the Weimar Republic. Nazi writing thus remained sealed off from contemporary literary developments abroad. Conversely Nazi authors had no influence outside the German-speaking lands. An example of the Nazi attitude towards aesthetic modernism can be seen in their campaign of vilification against Expressionism. Goebbels was in favour of certain artists on the grounds of their primitivism, their rebellion against materialism and their links with Germanic mysticism (not least, perhaps, because it was in Expressionism that his own literary roots lay). Rosenberg, on the other hand, condemned Expressionism outright and urged the adoption of neo-romantic or monumental neo-realist forms. Hitler himself always detested the Expressionists. Though some visual artists survived the first purge of decadent art in 1933, none escaped a second assault which began in 1936 and culminated in the notorious Exhibition of the following year. Many literary Expressionists had, of course, been associated with humanist or socialist values and were therefore condemned from the outset.[7] In the course of this campaign the Nazis turned their wrath on one of the foremost German poets of the twentieth century, Gottfried Benn, finally compelling him to 'emigrate'—as he called it—into that 'aristocratic' form of exile, the German army.

B. Gottfried Benn

The case of Gottfried Benn illustrates the susceptibility of certain intellectual circles to the appeal of fascism, and their subsequent disillusionment when it proved impossible to maintain any kind of intellectual independence or to pursue any literary development which did not accord with the tenets of the Nazi ideology and aesthetic.[8]

In the early twenties Benn had withdrawn into a nihilistic aestheticism. By the end of the decade his regressive irrationalism translated itself into an anti-Marxist polemic. Finally his aestheticism toppled over into a glorification of barbarity. In the first months of the Third Reich he proclaimed his commitment to the regime and attacked its opponents. Yet he was ignorant of much of the party programme, had never attended a political meeting or rally, and had not read *Mein Kampf*. In fact it was not political considerations in the narrower sense that determined his attitude but his fears of cultural disaster. He believed that rationalism had destroyed human values and the totality of nature. Western man was undergoing a process of progressive cerebration which threatened to culminate in his own extinction, with the rapidly multiplying peoples of Eastern Europe spilling over to take his place. The only power capable of transcending nihilism was artistic form: here was the affirmation that could bridge the abyss of violence, chaos, and contingency. How Benn came to identify this Nietzschean affirmation with the 'national revolution', to make the transition from a purely private response to a collective ideological solution which he had always spurned, can perhaps only be explained by the degree to which he had hitherto felt alienated and isolated in the society of his day. It was a precarious enough alliance but, while it lasted, fervently and zealously proclaimed.

Various speeches and addresses supported the regime against its liberal or socialist critics, and saluted its dynamism, its rediscovery of the mythic ground of Being.[9] But Benn still had to live down his suspect past: his aesthetic modernism. The only way to convince the regime of his reliability would have been to produce an appropriate literary work in full accordance with the new cultural policy, as Johst and Bronnen did. But this contribution Benn could not make. He had nothing but contempt for Nazi literature. His reputation therefore continued to bear the stigma of '*entartete Kunst*', though in a defence of Expressionism he did try to present it as an Aryan phenomenon fully compatible with National Socialism. At one point he was accused of being a Jew and forced to establish his racial credentials in public. But his cosmic pessimism was hardly attuned to the millennium which had just dawned. And his idea that creative genius went hand in hand with physiological decadence was closer to turn-of-the-century aestheticism than to the heroism of the new era. Many of his theories were too esoteric or recondite for comfort. By August 1934 Benn was admitting in private his thorough disenchantment with the Third Reich. The *putsch* against Röhm and the S.A. had been the last straw. Early in 1935 he rejoined the Army. It was only his good relations with his military superiors (and their distaste for the Party) which enabled him to survive the attacks on him in the S.S. journal and the *Völkischer Beobachter* in 1936. The campaign was renewed the following year in a book bearing the eloquent title *Säuberung des Kunsttempels* and finally in March 1938 he was expelled from the *Reichsschrifttumskammer* and forbidden to publish.

Benn's reaction to the disappointment of his political hopes had been once again to endeavour to separate entirely the spheres of spirit and power, a distinction for which he had argued in his polemic against left-wing committed writing in the last years of the Republic. This apparently so modern poet fell back on a familiar tradition once his brief outburst of political radicalism had spent itself.

C. The 'innere Emigration'

Not all the literature written in Hitler's Germany was Nazi-inspired or crypto-fascist. Between 1933 and 1935 some one hundred contributions by members of the *Bund proletarisch-revolutionärer Schriftsteller* were smuggled out of Germany to appear in the *Neue Deutsche Blätter* in Prague. One of the Berlin leaders of the *Bund* was Jan Petersen. His chronicle *Unsere Strasse* was sent to Czechoslovakia and published in Berne, Moscow and London. It was the only work written inside the Third Reich which directly depicted the resistance struggle. There was, too, a literature of the camps and prisons ranging from anonymous verses to sonnet cycles, from Werner Krauss' novel *PLN* to private letters.[10] But the phenomenon known as the '*innere Emigration*' implies a different kind of writer and a different kind of experience.[11]

There were many conservative writers such as Hans Carossa or Ernst Wiechert who chose to remain in Nazi Germany, not necessarily because they were impressed by the Führer personally or by his policies, but because they saw the impetus behind the national movement as a token of moral renewal. National Socialism was able to tap a vast reserve of idealistic passion among the bourgeois intelligentsia who heard only the high-minded clichés and ignored the sordid, brutal political realities. There was an initial identity of interest between conservative writers and the Nazis in that the conservatives shared their dislike of aesthetic modernism, their hostility towards the alleged materialism of modern civilization, their contempt for liberalism and a vulgar hedonism, their fear of social anarchy and nihilism. Moreover some conservatives were prone to glorify Prussianism and patriotic sentiment. Where the conservative writers differed from the Nazis was in the matter of basic values and the solutions they proposed. Instead of the abolition of class conflict in a total mobilization of society, they postulated the return of social harmony through a hierarchic structure based on estates. Instead of totalitarian subordination to the will of one man and one ideology, they advocated a semi-feudal authoritarianism. Instead of a message of hatred and violence, they preached a return to traditional moral values and brotherly love. Instead of the will to power, they urged detachment from the things of this world and a cultivation of inwardness. Instead of biological racialism, they endorsed a spiritual elitism.

Clearly the differences between the conservative intellectuals and men like Jünger or Benn, to say nothing of Rosenberg or Goebbels, were enormous. What is remarkable is the degree to which these differences were obscured or ignored in the common struggle against rationalism, Marxism, decadence and liberal society. The conservatives were so imbued with the Idealist tradition, so unaccustomed to political analysis and ignorant of the possibilities and limitations of political systems, that they were easily deceived by a semantic confidence trick. They believed in the rhetoric and silently acquiesced in the tactics. They recognized the signals of a common heritage and purpose, and dismissed any contrary indications as unfortunate excesses or deviations. Only after the Nazis came to power and the full implications of totalitarian rule made themselves felt did German conservatives begin to feel uneasy. It took a lost war finally to impel them into abortive action or clandestine commitment.

The notion of an '*innere Emigration*' became an issue immediately after the Second World War, particularly as a result of the public correspondence between Frank Thiess and Thomas Mann.[12] The often vituperative debate revolved around such questions as whether everything written within Nazi Germany represented a token of acquiescence in the regime; or was it possible to have published without compromising one's integrity? Was everything that did not oppose Nazism necessarily its ally? Or had an intellectual resistance existed? There is little point in reopening the argument on the level of personalities or of sweeping moral judgments. But it is worthwhile looking back to the situation which gave rise to the controversy.

The term '*innere Emigration*' has always been somewhat elastic; it has been applied to a variety of attitudes ranging from courageous resistance to gross opportunism, from total silence to veiled criticism. As a term of literary history the concept is most usefully reserved for those writers who overtly and expressly distanced themselves from the regime and who propounded their opposing values in full awareness of their political implications. The possibilities for expressing dissent were of course extremely limited. The disciples of inwardness had no conception of the extent to which the totalitarian state would control the hearts and minds of its citizens. Writers whose whole philosophy was based on the separation of politics and literature, of Life and Spirit, of Caesar and God, awoke to the realization that all intellectual activity was now politicized. Nothing was passed for publication which did not seem useful to the regime, however indirectly. Naturally the censors made mistakes, and conflict between rival organs of the State and the Party undermined the system's efficiency in this as in other spheres, but a writer who wished to communicate his dissent could not count on the fallibility of the functionaries responsible for reading his manuscript. In practice he was left with three choices. He could adopt a highly oblique method of criticism such as allegory, parable, fable or historical analogy; or he could circulate his work clandestinely, which for practical reasons meant poems or pamphlets; or he could publish abroad under a pseudonym. If the last two methods were fraught with personal danger (to his credit, Werner Bergengruen used both), the first ran the risk of being ignored or misinterpreted by virtue of its very indirectness. It has been claimed that people became adept at reading between the lines and attuned to the accents of the 'language of slavery',[13] through which critics of the regime communicated with each other without betraying themselves to the dictators. But if the *Sklavensprache* had to be camouflaged beneath the language of the masters, was it always so easy to distinguish between the true and the false? Could the dissenters disguise their purpose in this way without radically modifying their aims? Was the price they paid in order to appear at all—too great? For all the veiled criticism in Bergengruen's *Der Grosstyrann und das Gericht* the novel won Party approval as a glorification of the 'leadership principle', while the fervent Prussian ethos of Jochen Klepper's novel about Frederick William I, *Der Vater* (1937), ensured its official promotion despite its equally intransigent Protestantism. One commentator concludes that with the best will in the world the writers of the *'innere Emigration'* 'involuntarily helped the regime to build up a facade of spiritual freedom and cultural continuity in spite of the concentration camps . . . In this way they were integrated into the collective organization and, in effect, strengthened it'.[14] What is certain is that even when the *'innere Emigration'* spoke with an unequivocal voice, it never transcended the fateful errors which had led to its predicament in the first place.

The literary forms favoured by these writers were the novel and the lyric. The drama, which required a public forum, was virtually closed to them. Above all they cultivated historical fiction, for in the past they could rediscover a clear design and a human autonomy which the present denied. Or, to view it more negatively, one could say that they fled from a confused, unyielding present reality that seemed to shatter their image of man and his world to historical material which they could mould according to a preconceived and comforting pattern. Nazi writers sometimes resorted to the historical novel in order to glorify a heroic model and to seek historical sanctions for Germany's current destiny. Non-political authors turned to 'antiquarian' *pointillisme* and romanticized biography for light relief. But the conservative religious writers of the *'innere Emigration'* sought out the past in order to find parallels that demonstrated man's weakness, guilt and presumption, his need of divine mercy, and his ability to find redemption. (Hence, for instance, Gertrud von Le Fort's *Die Magdeburgische Hochzeit* or Stefan Andres' *El Greco malt den Grossinquisitor* or Reinhold Schneider's *Las Casas vor Karl V.*) But since they lacked political or historical insight into their own times, they found it difficult to discover an adequate equivalent in the past, and much of their writing seems curiously beside the point. By viewing events *sub specie aeternitatis* they attributed them solely to moral decisions and posited remedies for social evils in the spiritual conversion of individuals, especially those in positions of power. In this respect they repeated the historical error of the 'rhetorical' Expressionists, as exemplified in Kaiser's *Die Bürger von Calais* or Hasenclever's *Antigone*. Later, particularly during the War, when the intractable corruption of Germany's leaders had become only too clear, history was transformed into apocalypse and the sole remaining hope was seen to reside in God's mercy. What is missing from this writing is any impulse to social revolution: its attitude to rebellion is determined by Luther's interpretation of Romans XIII (the powers that be are ordained of God . . .).[15]

Not surprisingly the search for design and meaning is reflected in the poetic forms favoured by the conservative writers, above all the sonnet.[16] The sonnet was 'untimely' in more senses than one in Nazi Germany. It was a strenuously classical form far removed from hymns to the Führer or S.A. marching songs; and it was an alien, non-Germanic form equally remote from the romantic *Lied* and the Wagnerian *Stabreim*. The choice of poetic medium was thus itself an implicit gesture of dissent, at least against the official aesthetic. The sonnet was used in a firmly traditional manner, with no attempt at either structural or linguistic experiment. Its strictness, discipline and clarity convey, like the recourse to historical fiction, the desire to affirm an absolute law that controls and shapes a chaotic material world. Behind this formalism lies a strange paradox. Emigré writers were beginning to despair of the power of art to achieve any impact in the real world: but the writers of the '*innere Emigration*' who were compelled to witness the daily repudiation of all their most cherished values clung to their belief in the moral influence of artistic form and to a Johannine interpretation of the Word. It was not simply the desire for didactic clarity that accounted for the absence of innovation, but rather their unquestioning faith in an older heritage, an older language even—in short, in an Idealist equivalence of world and word. Through language and art they tried to counteract the process of brutalization and distortion. Yet all too often they remained imprisoned within a highly stylized convention, suffused with archaic or idyllic elements and pseudo-Biblical pathos.

What function did such writing fulfil? It was produced for an educated middle-class readership, a group of like-minded people who found themselves involved in a political process of which they disapproved but which they were helpless to change. This conservative literature sought to reassure and console by invoking the ultimate victory of the spiritual principle. Although the explicitly critical writing circulated privately, often in verse form, among small groups and in a local area, the more indirect expressions of dissent which appeared in print attracted a large following. The appeal was partly escapist, partly compensatory, and in human terms it is easily understood. In political terms, however, it was little short of disastrous. While it reinforced the prejudices that had originally led to Hitler's electoral successes, it obscured the question of specific responsibility by hypostasizing the theme of guilt into the myth of original sin. Instead of trying to understand how evil had taken on the particular form of National Socialism or how the Nazis had come to dominate German society, the '*innere Emigration*' contented itself with proclaiming the sinfulness of the whole of mankind. By demonizing Hitler into an embodiment of Satanic power, it neglected to study the all-too-human social and economic process that had brought him to the fore. In short, it was informed by a fatalism no less insidious than that of a Jünger or a Benn. And in a world which demanded that they rethink their faith, their philosophy, above all their attitude towards evil, these conservative writers proved incapable of learning from their experience.

An early example of this failure can be found in Werner Bergengruen's novel *Der Grosstyrann und das Gericht* (1935). Set in Renaissance Italy, it relates the search for the murderer of a high official amid an atmosphere of corrosive fear, greed, suspicion and betrayal. Yet after confusion and violence appear to have shattered the divine order and beauty of the world, the reality of God's mercy is reasserted. In its reflections upon the relationship between justice and power, the novel evinces an idealism which sanctions political activity only in the execution of a higher spiritual purpose and which disparages a more pragmatic view of politics as mechanical and bureaucratic. By dint of ignoring the implications of the inevitable disparity between might and right, Bergengruen lapses into a pious optimism which flies in the face of all the evidence of his own age. Logically he faces a choice between the tragedy of moral compromise or the martyrdom of the intransigent idealist. The unreal alternative which in fact he offers, a vision of earthly and divine power reconciled through the conversion of the hubristic despot, was irrelevant to the situation of 1935 and could only have encouraged a retreat into inwardness on the part of those who contemplated the desolate political vista of their age.

Much of the Christian writing of the '*innere Emigration*' is armoured against experience in a highly questionable manner. The victory of the Cross is hollow indeed unless it encompasses and transcends the full measure of anguish, suffering and despair. It is not the religious optimism in itself that is suspect but the ease with which it is invoked. Like others of their generation with very different moral values, these writers betray a terrifying failure of imagination in the face of the unprecedented disaster all around them. All too often their vocabulary and imagery convey not so much a living experience as a defence against it.

Another instructive example of the limits of the '*innere Emigration*' is provided by Ernst Wiechert who enjoyed a considerable literary following during the Third Reich. He also earned the unenviable distinction of being one of the few writers to survive a period of correction in a concentration camp.[17] His experiences in Buchenwald were recorded in *Der Totenwald*, written in 1939 and buried in his garden until after the War. For all its sententiousness and rhetorical pathos, the book remains a sombre record of his shame at having compromised with the regime, and of the barbaric circumstances of his imprisonment, a dark night of the soul illuminated only by the humanity of fellow prisoners who helped him to survive, many of them Communists.

In 1939, however, Wiechert's overt literary activity took the form of a novel called *Das einfache Leben* which offered a seductive escapist alternative. It was eagerly seized on by his readers, for over a quarter of a million copies were sold in two years.[18] The book is a mixture of utopianism and mawkishness with a strong undercurrent of depressing nature philosophy. It issues in an uncritical fatalism, all-affirming, anti-individualist and regressive. Again one cannot but wonder at its sheer irrelevance to the problems that it is ostensibly meant to resolve: the final decline of a military and feudal society, the advent of a modern industrial culture and, by implication, the development of totalitarianism. There is an inherent falseness in the advice of landowners and *rentiers* that one should resort to honest toil as the solution to all ills. There is a despairing helplessness in their propounding of duty and diligence when the ultimate meaning of their existence has been called into question. Instead of grappling with the uncertainties, conflicts and complexities of modern life the hero can only retreat into a simplicity and 'authenticity' the desire for which had already played a fateful part in the calamity of 1933. The religious affirmation in which his story culminates turns out to be an atheism that lacks the courage of its convictions: for the law which he acknowledges is nothing less than 'the final absurdity of existence', glossed over by sentimental remnants of traditional piety. Small wonder if in the face of these confusions, this incipient nihilism, Orla's favourite image is that of the 'stone on the river bed', the pre-conscious mineral stillness at the heart of the natural world. It is the last escape of all.

Ernst Jünger represents a third possibility of the '*innere Emigration*': aristocratic detachment. When the reality of the Third Reich became clear to him, his natural elitism reasserted itself and he remained aloof from the vulgarity and crudeness of those whom he had helped to achieve power. Only once did he indicate in public his attitude to the regime, in the novel *Auf den Marmorklippen* (1939). The implications of the book were eagerly discussed at the time in the circles of the '*innere Emigration*' (though advertisements for the book were forbidden, it sold well over 10,000 copies by 1940).[19] After the War apologists spoke of a bold gesture of resistance. This allegory of the rise of fascist terror in a decadent world shows the narrator's sanctuary threatened by the encroaching powers of a sinister *Oberförster*. The marble cliffs have eventually to be abandoned and a new life sought in exile. But the central message of the book lies in the experience of inner victory, the triumph of the spirit over instinct, adversity, pain and fear. This was the strength of the Mauretanian elite when the narrator belonged to their number: the stillness in their souls as in the heart of a cyclone. This too is what validates the death of a young prince—the quiet smile of serenity that betokens the casting aside of weakness and the revelation of the 'great order' of Being. Inspired by this sight (on a severed head) the narrator declares that it is better to die with the free than to march in triumph with the slaves. The book envisages no possibility of defeating the *Oberförster* by political or military means and indeed suggests that this is irrelevant, provided the struggle gives one the chance to attain the necessary sublimity. Moreover, the novel is ethically flawed, in that the victory over fear appears to be synonymous with a victory over all feeling. The stillness at the heart of the cyclone denotes not only indifference to one's own suffering but an aesthetic detachment from the anguish of others. The narrator's principal response to the rule of the *Oberförster* is one of repugnance. At best he experiences a fleeting moment of sadness as when he glimpses the prince's mutilated features. But in general the book gives the impression of feeling rigidly controlled or suppressed. A cool, impersonal style fails to capture any sense of the moment. At one point there occurs a revealing statement that like the cosmos the human world must necessarily be engulfed in flames from time to time in order to purge and renew itself. The *Oberförster* and his rule of terror are symptoms of just such a periodic holocaust which the narrator observes with acquiescent, clinical interest.

Chapter Five
The Literature of Exile

The event which precipitated the flight of so many intellectuals from Germany was the Reichstag fire of 27 February 1933.[1] The Nazis used the fire as a pretext to round up their opponents, who included not only the Communists but anyone known for his anti-nationalist or pro-democratic views. Ossietzky, Mühsam, Renn, Bredel, Seghers, Kisch and Hiller were among those arrested. By the autumn of 1933 all the significant emigré writers were out of Germany. Scarcely any had taken care to transfer funds while they still had the opportunity or made mental preparation for going into exile. And to begin with, few believed that the extraordinary situation would last.

The exiled writers were a motley band.[2] Some had left because of their political views, others for racial reasons, many for both. A few were non-political modernists who left in pursuit of aesthetic freedom. Ideologically they included Communists, Social Democrats, non-party left-wing radicals, liberals, monarchists, even national revolutionaries. These divisions in turn produced a variety of interpretations of the Third Reich. The conflicts of the republican era continued in exile, exacerbated by the consciousness of defeat and the search for scapegoats. The financial resources of the exiles varied enormously, a factor which was important in determining the different treatment meted out to them by their 'host' countries. As the emigrés spread out all over Europe and beyond, they shared only a common predicament: that of writers who overnight had been deprived of their natural readers or audiences and cut off from the living community whose language they wrote. The need to produce work that would sell in translation combined with their sense of having to preserve a national heritage and encouraged a conservatism of form and language. A writer like Musil who resolutely pursued his modernist experimental fiction was dependent on private charity.

The popularity of historical fiction inside the Third Reich was paralleled among exiled writers such as the Mann brothers, Lion Feuchtwanger and Stefan Zweig—and for similar reasons, sometimes escapist, sometimes didactic. Likewise the sonnet form was cultivated not only inside Germany but also—improbably—in Moscow by Johannes R. Becher, who turned his hand to this and other classical forms.

One can distinguish between three broad categories of response to the challenge of exile. The first was fatalistic and escapist (the flight of Döblin or Werfel into Catholicism, mysticism and inwardness). The second response came from those writers who concentrated on preserving a humanist and liberal heritage, the ideals of the two Weimars, and who, although opposed to Hitler, resisted the calls for a committed art in an agitatory sense. Unlike the Communists, for example, they did not participate in everyday political activity, nor did they support any particular party or organization. The third kind of writer was actively anti-fascist, continuing the struggle from other European countries and later from the Americas. (Among this category one might include Toller, Joseph Roth, Heinrich Mann and the KPD authors.) In the early years many exiled German authors sought to enlighten the world as to what was happening inside Germany and to warn of the threat to the rest of Europe: hence Feuchtwanger's exposure of anti-semitism and *Gleichschaltung* in his novel *Die Geschwister Oppenheim* (1933).[3] The Communist activists even tried to keep up contact with the socialist underground, such as it was, and to smuggle writing both in and out of the Reich. A series of left-wing novels described the struggle of the resistance groups in an optimistic spirit, in the deluded belief that the regime would itself soon bring about a decisive swing to the left among the proletariat. As late as 1935 Communist exiles in particular still expected the imminent collapse of National Socialism either through violent uprising or through its own inherent weaknesses. There is, however, a noticeable difference in Anna Segher's *Das siebte Kreuz* (1939) which no longer maintains the fiction that any organized opposition survives within the Reich and which holds up the moral commitment of individuals as the only hope for the future. In the late thirties, as the regime consolidated its hold and the international community accepted fascism as a *fait accompli* or even welcomed it, the emigrés experienced disillusionment and a growing sense of futility. With the outbreak of the War and the early German successes, a second wave of emigration spilled out of Europe and a series of suicides charted the fear and despair that dogged the footsteps of so many exiled intellectuals. Even committed writers saw their activism apparently rendered irrelevant.

The year 1933, however, marked a far less decisive point in the *literary* development of many writers[4] than the hiatus in their private lives suggests. For in the second half of the twenties a reaction against the laconic matter-of-factness and exclusively social themes of objectivism, or against left-wing demands for commitment, had already made itself felt in various ways among bourgeois writers. There was a rediscovery of the natural world and a nostalgic return to the past or the private self. Some explored the realms of myth, legend and mysticism. These tendencies were reinforced in exile, so that writers like Thomas Mann or Roth could reconcile their anti-fascist publicistic activity with the exploration of artistic worlds far removed from the sphere of 'telegrams and anger'.

1. Bertolt Brecht: *Mutter Courage und ihre Kinder* (1941)

Cut off after 1933 from a readily available theatrical context, from a rapport with a familiar audience, Brecht found it difficult to discover an appropriate form for the directly activist pieces which he continued to write in exile and which remain relative failures. A measure of detachment from the immediate struggle was necessary before he could begin to strike the right note, whether in the reflective ironies of the *Flüchtlingsgespräche*, the lyricism of the Svendborg poems, or the dramatic achievement of the major plays. In these latter works the immediate political conflict receded into the background and Brecht emerged as a Marxist *moraliste*, articulating problems of human behaviour and exploring the possibilities of human freedom within the framework of a materialist interpretation of consciousness and society.

The opening scene of Brecht's play *Mutter Courage und ihre Kinder* which is set in the Thirty Years War contains in essence the theme of the action as a whole: Mother Courage's attempt to live off war without giving it anything in return. The purpose of Mother Courage's career as a canteen owner and camp-follower is to sustain and preserve her family. Yet by the end of the play that career has destroyed the very thing it is meant to protect. Again and again her commercial instinct causes her to neglect her children and to hasten their death. Mother Courage is as much a victim of war as a parasite on it. This hard, experienced, worldly-wise woman fails to see the one simple truth about her position: that the means of life have become the ends, and that life itself is the sufferer. And all the time it is her mute daughter Kattrin who witnesses and experiences this truth.

Inarticulate and timid, cut off from ordinary social relationships, Kattrin has not developed a protective skin between herself and the world. The vein of feeling throbs only just beneath the surface. She responds directly and instinctively to the spectacle of suffering and anguish, amid a society conditioned to ignore them in the interests of survival. She is the most important single instrument of *Verfremdung* in the play, for by observing her reaction to events we ourselves are made to see afresh the consequences of her mother's indifference to pain and deprivation. When a Catholic army prepares to attack Halle, Kattrin achieves a moral freedom and a chance to act which have hitherto been denied her. What begins as another impulsive reaction becomes a conscious decision. As the intimidated peasants pray and throw themselves (and those about to be slaughtered) on God's mercy, Kattrin climbs on to a stable roof from where, in defiance of all threats and entreaties, she drums out a warning to the unsuspecting town. Although she is shot, the sleeping garrison is roused to the danger and Halle repulses the attackers. The virtues of her two brothers (honesty and boldness) were heavily qualified in our eyes by their deaths: her quality of compassion and self-sacrifice is validated by the saving of the town.

If ever proof were needed that Brecht's 'epic' theatre did not aim at excluding emotion or that the emotion did not creep in inadvertently, the final scene of the play provides it. The poignancy of Mother Courage's loss is not diminished by the reminders of her incorrigible shortsightedness. Conversely the sight of her grief and her resilience does not weaken our conviction of her personal responsibility. Sympathy and critical detachment merge in the indictment of a system which reduces everything to a price and perverts even the best in man. For whenever men behave in a harsh, stupid or cowardly fashion in the play, it is invariably in defence of their material welfare. Only Kattrin overcomes this material compulsion.

It was not important that Mother Courage should learn her lesson, commented Brecht, provided that the audience learnt theirs.[5] What the play tells us is that wars are instigated by the ruling class for the sake of their personal power and gain. That ideological crusades are a smokescreen for political ambitions. That bourgeois 'virtues' are a luxury which no poor man can afford in a society built on acquisition and exploitation. That in such a society love is a dangerous folly which only makes one easier to exploit. That the ordinary people upon whom the mighty depend for their subjects, soldiers or congregations are always the losers. But the mighty do not live for ever. True, it is pointless to rebel unless your wrath is strong enough (and cunning enough) to sustain you. Yet you cannot escape the consequences of the system by hoping to find a safe and comfortable niche. What then is to be done?

Mother Courage and Kattrin embody two possible responses to the world as they find it. The mother consistently points out that the individual must submit to social pressures. Kattrin in her own small way does something to change society. Both options demand their penalties. But whereas Mother Courage thrives on suffering and destruction, Kattrin prevents it. What is equally instructive is the manner in which her sacrifice is presented. The conventional Idealist associations—nobility, dignity, sublimity—are absent. In their place we see an example of suffering humanity driven to desperation, a half-demented, frightened, sobbing girl who knows only that if *she* submits to coercion, the children in the town will die. The literature of inwardness cannot muster a single instance of sacrifice that speaks to us so vividly and so directly. Brecht does not suggest that Kattrin's actions are the sole means of changing the world. But hers is a symbolic gesture which emphasizes the moral commitment that is essential if anything is to be changed. (Hence too Brecht's modified conception of Galileo in another play of these years: from approval of his pliability to a dialectical critique of his cowardice and compromise.) In the long run, the play implies, change can only come from those who have taken the measure of society like Mother Courage but do not share her greed and capitulation. It can come only from those who have it in them to emulate Kattrin's commitment at critical moments but who also possess the insight into social mechanisms which she lacks.

2. Thomas Mann: *Doktor Faustus* (1947)

Thomas Mann's initial reaction to the 'seizure of power' was an attitude of wait-and-see. On his children's insistence he did not return to Germany from a lecture tour abroad. But in the autumn of 1933 he went so far as to try and rid himself of the suspicion of anti-fascist activity by dissociating himself from the journal *Die Sammlung* edited by his son Klaus. Silence seemed to Mann the best way of maintaining contact with his public inside Germany. Gradually he realised that he had no choice but to commit himself openly, and from early in 1936 he became an unrelenting opponent of the Hitler regime. This activism was clearly a condition of his being able to remain (in Hölderlin's words) a *Dichter in dürft'ger Zeit*. On the eve of the Second World War the policies of appeasement and non-involvement, the suspicion encountered by many German refugees abroad, and the pro-fascist sympathies in several Western states helped to radicalize Mann's ideas. Later still, as the truth about Nazi atrocities became known, the emigré intellectuals were caught up in the endless debate about collective guilt and in speculation about whether the Nazi crimes were an inevitable outcome of the character and traditions of the German people. Mann now turned away from an economic explanation of Hitler's power to a study of the German soul.

At the heart of his complex and profound novel *Doktor Faustus* lies the parallelism between Mann's hero, the composer Adrian Leverkühn, and the German nation. The artistic dilemma which prompts Adrian into concluding a pact with the Devil is the failure of true inspiration. What the Devil offers as a substitute for sterile reflectiveness and inhibiting intellectualism is an experience of holy fire that has long been wanting, a rapture, an enthusiasm which God—with his predilection for rationality—can no longer supply; it means freedom from doubt, a compulsive dictation which presents no choices and needs no revision. Modern art seeks inspiration not only for formal or aesthetic reasons. It is also trying to overcome its isolation from the rest of society. Adrian longs for a new innocence, serenity and humility in which art will once again find itself in the service of a whole community or some sort of higher order, a *Verband* or *re-ligio*. The crisis of modern art is paralleled by the decline of bourgeois humanism, the end of a secular, rationalist tradition whose political precipitate was liberal democracy. The loss of creative inspiration is matched by the disappearance of the sense of wholeness in the bourgeois order, by the corrosive scepticism towards its staple values. The charge of mechanical intellectualism here raised against modern art was frequently levelled at Weimar Germany's experiment in liberal democracy; the corresponding fear that pluralism would lead to anarchy, another commonplace of intellectual conservatism, is echoed in Adrian's fear of artistic licence and unbridled subjectivity. In the conversations of the Munich intellectuals of the Weimar era we see Leverkühn's sublime yearnings translated into the base coinage of political slogans. Here the cult of violence, vitalism and myth echoes Adrian's desire for a new *Kultus*, a new barbarism. If the Munich intellectuals show the bizarre degeneration of the Idealist tradition, Adrian embodies the related aesthetic cult of inwardness with its supreme achievements and its terrible human cost. Even the narrator, Adrian's life-long and tragically unrequited friend Serenus Zeitblom, shows the susceptibility and confusion to which contemporary German humanism is prone: as the supreme representative in literature of the 'internal emigration', Zeitblom periodically betrays the ambiguities of his patriotic pride and the insidious influences of the ruling ideology on his thinking. It is not until well into the novel, as the horrors perpetrated by the regime become clear even to an unworldly scholar, that Zeitblom pronounces his first anathema.

Leverkühn's quest for a way out of his artistic dilemma takes him into a union with the demonic. What the pact with the Devil symbolizes— if indeed it is merely symbolic[6]—is a surrender to monstrous, destructive forces, to primeval, bloodstained irrationalism, to frenzy and pain, to the dark chthonic powers underlying the phenomenal world. Paradoxically the surrender to the demonic is dictated not by the abandonment of spirituality but by Adrian's determined pursuit of it. In the absoluteness of his commitment, the spirit devours itself in a desperate attempt to achieve self-realization. Adrian Leverkühn succumbs to a blasphemous Messianism which pursues salvation through evil and transgresses in order to redeem. Apostasy becomes a perverse act of faith. For just as the musical tradition has declined into a set of empty formulae; just as the era of bourgeois liberalism is felt to have degenerated into mechanical expediency, so too religious faith is taken so much for granted that it has grown hollow and inconsequential. The mind charged with spiritual yearning cannot find fulfilment in conventional religious forms but must turn to the demonic for succour. So too Germany's 'breakthrough' of 1914, motivated primarily (it is claimed) by the spiritual imperatives of sacrifice, expiation and entry into a higher order of being, justified for Zeitblom all offences against ordinary morality; and Adrian, like his diabolic mentor, accepts that the price of supreme achievement may be what run-of-the-mill ethics would call criminality. This self-appointed redeemer borrows the Superman's licence to transcend the restraints and inhibitions of a cowardly world—and here again forges a link between his proud isolation and the national community in which he lives.

The inspiration of Adrian's music is almost always nihilistic and destructive. With his final masterpiece, the Lamentation of Doctor Faustus, Leverkühn sets out to 'take back', to negate or revoke the Ninth Symphony and the Ode to Joy. It is a complete repudiation of the divine in the world, an ultimate confession of spiritual anguish that can be neither healed nor assuaged. Leverkühn's spirituality survives only in the intensity of his blasphemy, in the idea of a 'supreme, self-validating strenuousness' which has been seen as the hallmark of his age.[7] The 'breakthrough' which he ultimately achieves at the cost of his soul drives him forward into nothingness.

And yet a question mark remains. At the conclusion of his Faust oratorio one group of instruments after another falls silent until only a single 'cello note is left to die slowly away. That final note of despair seems (we are told) to become transformed in the listener into a glimmer of hope—the hope that despair may be transcended through a miracle that surpasses all understanding and even the doctrines of faith itself. For by the end, in a state of deepest attrition, Adrian has utterly renounced the demonic alliance, even though he believes repentance can no longer save him. Instead of hazarding everything on the return of inspiration, he tells his audience, one should strive

> klug zu sorgen, was vonnöten auf Erden, damit es dort besser werde, und besonnen dazu zu tun, dass unter den Menschen solche Ordnung sich herstelle, die dem schönen Werk wieder Lebensgrund und ein redlich Hineinpassen bereiten . . .[8]
>
> *(to attend to what is needful on earth, that things may get better there, and prudently to toil for the establishment of a human order which will prepare a living foundation for the work of beauty and a just place in the affairs of men . . .)*

At the last he repudiates the aestheticism which had led him to value the artistic 'breakthrough' above all else and to divorce his art from humanitarian values. And he appeals in effect for men to work towards a just social order that will provide a proper basis for the work of art, an appropriate setting for the *re-ligio* which he himself had pursued through demonic means. The political corollary is intimated in the contrast between the compassion and charity of Frau Schweigestill, the country woman in whose farmhouse Adrian has sought refuge (did not the Devil concede that he was not one of her kind?) and the indifference, discomfiture, unfeeling curiosity or moral indignation of the bourgeois intellectuals whom Adrian is addressing.

The novel attempts to give the lie once and for all to the notion of a *Geist* that is devoid of sensuality, of an art that inhabits a socio-political vacuum. It offers a critique of the Idealist cult of inwardness at the very point when historical pressures drive it to seek reintegration with the community. It shows that if the values of inwardness and aestheticism are simply transferred to the social dimension, their absolute, uncompromising intensity are fraught with disaster. The condition of 'coldness' which Adrian takes upon himself is a poetic cypher for the inability of the exclusively aesthetic imagination to accommodate the human qualities of love, care and compassion. The temperament which views the world as an aesthetic phenomenon sees life merely as the material of art. That life has its own priorities and its own intrinsic values which may be at odds with the demands of art—this the aesthetic mind cannot comprehend. But its own pretensions are based on an illusion: pure *Geist* is a misconception, for art and life are interdependent. When Adrian concludes a pact with the Devil, he sacrifices his soul and his emotions to the future of his art, a truly aesthetic renunciation. The equivalent in the socio-political sphere is the vision of dreamers, artists and philosophers who seek to shape society to their abstract designs. The sheer intransigence of their unworldly vision overrides all proper considerations, subordinating everything to the realization of the ideal and justifying every means by reference to the spiritual end. Just such an abstract idealism we can observe in the Munich intellectuals and behind them in a host of German writers from the Romantics to Gottfried Benn. In the terrifying ease with which it succumbs to barbarity, aestheticism—one way and another—pronounces sentence on itself.

A central problem remains. Are the two areas of experience, the aesthetic and the political, compatible or commensurate throughout the novel? On one vital issue there exists a radical incongruence which ultimately makes us doubt the wisdom of Mann's choice of an artist figure as his representative hero. Although there is no doubt as to the human cost which Leverkühn inflicts on himself to achieve his purpose, although the moral nihilism of his music is manifest, we are confronted with the equally incontrovertible fact of his aesthetic achievement. Leverkühn does attain the longed-for 'breakthrough' from calculatory coldness into heartfelt expressiveness, and whatever fears and reservations his friend Zeitblom, the narrator, may harbour, he never allows them to invalidate his judgment of the music. The Lamentation of Doctor Faustus is described as the ultimate liberation, and Zeitblom even bases his hope of a religious paradox on the aesthetic paradox mirrored there. As total construction has given birth to authentic expression, so too salvation may yet emerge from the depths of godlessness.

But what social or political 'breakthrough' is comparable to the aesthetic fruits of Leverkühn's union with the demonic? What construction of the Third Reich can offer any matching achievement? What political liberty emerged under the tyranny of National Socialism to match the mystery of artistic freedom which is said to ensue from the formal *Gebundenbeit*, the total order and discipline, of the musical composition? Is there any parallel between Adrian's self-sacrifice for his art—and the hecatomb of Europe? Is the faint hope of redemption with which the novel closes, a prayer dictated by Mann's avowed love for his character, an appropriate response to the political catastrophe that now overshadows Leverkühn's personal fate? By focusing on the aesthetic dimension of the problem Mann ends up trapped by the conflict between moral and aesthetic values which he is trying to resolve. And though on one level Leverkühn's confession repudiates the primacy of art, the experience of his music leaves the problem as open as ever. The ambiguity may be justified in terms of our response to art but is surely inappropriate when transferred to the socio-political sphere where other values predominate. In this exhaustive critique of aestheticism Mann remains tragically enmeshed in the very tradition he is criticizing. His Faust bequeaths to us an *œuvre* which we are bound to judge aesthetically, not just morally or socially. The final conjunction of friend and fatherland is thus possible only in prayer. In symbolic terms—for here again we must judge aesthetically—the two are no longer commensurate.[9]

Conclusion

A generation of German writers who unlike many of their predecessors realized that their art could not ignore the political issues of their day found themselves on the brink of abandoning art altogether. The parties regarded literature at best as serving their ideology and at worst as a frivolous irrelevance. The writers for their part were aware that in seeking even a committed art they were already abstracting from immediate, concrete reality and subordinating it to alien laws, thus depriving themselves of the chance to influence the political situation directly. The dilemma of committed literature is the conflict between didacticism and aesthetic pleasure. The greater the claim of such writing to aesthetic recognition, the more extensively it assimilates historical reality to its own autonomous being. Though the aesthetic experience cannot ever be entirely separated from its historical context (language alone guarantees that link), it remains of a fundamentally different order from our political experience. Art loses the power to effect change in proportion to its transmutation of given historical data into the stuff of aesthetic creation, according to the conventions of its chosen form.[1] In the face of the historical crisis of the inter-war years, the temptation was to abandon literary creation altogether and to sacrifice art to activism, fiction to the documentary. Some writers maintained a productive tension between art and activism by drawing a distinction between their publicistic work and their creative writing, the latter manifesting a far greater degree of reflective detachment and complexity.

At either end of the ideological spectrum the pressure was towards collective art, an art which transcended the bourgeois heritage of individualism and articulated the needs and aspirations of whole social groups. Some of the techniques used and their consequences proved to be disconcertingly similar; the theatrical chorus, the exemplary hero whose private life is totally subordinate to the collective, the degeneration of character into caricature, a 'realism' which confuses the descriptive and the prescriptive, the cult of monumentality and heroicization, a bankruptcy of the imagination in the face of a barbaric reality. The further art progressed towards the collective, the closer it approximated to cultic ritual. Indeed the substitution of ideology for religion is a major feature of both right- and left-wing writing. One prime difference remains. Only Communist or Socialist writers chose to stress the typical by reference to historical, social and economic data, thus appealing to intellectual judgment. The more perceptive left-wing writers even presented their figures with ironic detachment—at least for as long as they were able to avoid the constraints of the Party aesthetic. Fascism, by contrast, uniformly demanded the elimination of the rational faculty and deplored narrative irony.

It was rare for a revolutionary political commitment to go hand in hand with a revolutionary aesthetic. The monolithic parties shared a profound mistrust of artistic innovation and based their own aesthetic canons on conservative premises. Critical thought, linguistic innovations, the very autonomy of the creative imagination were anathema to closed ideological systems designed to manipulate rather than to extend human consciousness. Moreover, the fundamental pessimism of modernist art offended the inherently positive direction of political ideologies. Fascism could accommodate the irrational anti-Enlightenment quality of modernism but not its anarchic destructiveness, its onslaught on traditional values, its subversion of the substance and meaning of the phenomenal world. Communism necessarily repudiated the legacy of irrationalism and equally rejected the modernist emphasis on existential solitude, the agonized isolation of the individual and the irreducible reality of pain and death. If the Communists tolerated the 'revolutionary' modernist,[2] they remained suspicious of his independent judgment and artistic freedom.

Enzensberger has argued that there is an indirect but inevitable connection between the poet's independence and originality in the use of language, and political subversion.[3] If we look at the *language* of poetry as well as at the political *opinions* of the poet, we see that there is no necessary correlation between the two. The conservative can seem revolutionary, the political radical a literary backwoodsman. It is shortsighted or even irrelevant to criticize writers for ignoring political themes—without at the same time considering the nature of their aesthetic achievement, their use of language and their impact on the sensibility of their readers. Viewed in this light, much of the political literature of our period seems overwhelmingly conservative. Paradoxically, the literature of Expressionism and Dada, however 'unpolitical' or historically ingenuous, may have achieved more by its revolutionary grammar than Brecht cared to admit. The real innovators, those writers who decisively rejected the forms and perspectives of the nineteenth century—Rilke, Kafka, Musil, for example—invariably lacked any creative interest in the *données* of the political world or any desire to become actively involved in the political struggle. A text which is committed to the critical elucidation of political issues and which manages to remain aesthetically interesting is relatively rare in the literature we have examined. The history of literary commitment in Germany during this period is all too often one of conflict, compromise, failure or delusion. The insidious corruption of the Lutheran and Idealist legacy is now patent. There were writers whose culpability is a matter of historical record. There were those who kept the memory of decency alive. Few escaped the compulsions of an age whose 'cursed spite' invaded the last sanctuaries of inwardness and finally exploded the myth of the non-political German.

Notes

Introduction

1. Ralf Dahrendorf, *Gesellschaft und Demokratie in Deutschland* (München, 1965), especially 'Der Unpolitische Deutsche'. For a fuller treatment of this subject, see my article 'Writers and Politics: Some Reflections on a German Tradition', *Journal of European Studies*, vol. vi, no. 2 (June 1976).

2. In 'Die Deutsche Literatur [im Ausland seit 1933]. Ein Dialog zwischen Politik and Kunst', now in *Aufsätze zur Literatur* (Olten/Freiburg i.B., 1963).

3. See Reinhold Aris, *History of Political Thought in Germany from 1789 to 1815* (London, 1936); G. P. Gooch, *Germany and the French Revolution*, 2nd Edn. (London, 1965); Hajo Holborn, 'Der deutsche Idealismus in sozialgeschichtlicher Beleuchtung', *Historische Zeitschrift*, vol. CLXXIV (October 1952), pp. 359–85.

4. See the two anthologies edited with excellent introductions by Jost Hermand: *Das Junge Deutschland* and *Der deutsche Vormärz* (Stuttgart, 1966 and 1967).

5. See Fritz Stern, 'The Political Consequences of the Unpolitical German' in *The Failure of Illiberalism. Essays on the Political Culture of Modern Germany* (London, 1972).

6. Roy Pascal, *From Naturalism to Expressionism. German Literature and Society 1880–1918* (London, 1973), p. 11.

7. *Ibid.*, pp. 102–3.

8. *Ibid.*, p. 105 and Friedrich Albrecht, *Deutsche Schriftsteller in der Entscheidung. Wege zur Arbeiterklasse 1918–1933* (Berlin/Weimar, 1970), p. 33.

9. Fritz Stern, *The Politics of Cultural Despair. A Study in the Rise of the Germanic Ideology* (Berkeley and Los Angeles, 1961), p. 208.

10. Max Weber, 'Politik als Beruf' [1918/19] in *Gesammelte Politische Schriften*, J. Winckelmann (ed.), 2nd Edn. (Tübingen, 1958), p. 541 and Heine, *Zur Geschichte der Religion und Philosophie in Deutschland*, C. P. Magill (ed.) (London, 1947), pp. 174–6.

Chapter One

1. See Kurt Sontheimer, *Antidemokratisches Denken in der Weimarer Republik. Die politischen Ideen des deutschen Nationalismus zwischen 1918 und 1933* (München, 1964), Chapter 5, 'Das Kriegserlebnis des Ersten Weltkrieges'; Rolf Geissler, *Dekadenz und Heroismus. Zeitroman und völkisch-nationalsozialistische Literaturkritik* (Stuttgart, 1964), pp. 76–103; Ernst Loewy, *Literatur unterm Hakenkreuz. Das Dritte Reich und seine Dichtung: eine Dokumentation*, Fischer-Bücherei 1042 (Frankfurt/Hamburg, 1969), 'Der militante Nationalismus'; Ernst Keller, *Nationalismus und Literatur* (Bern/München, 1970), esp. 'Langemarck'.

2. See J. P. Stern, 'The Dear Purchase', *The German Quarterly*, vol. XLI, no. 3 (May, 1968), pp. 317–40.

3. For a wider critical assessment of E.J.'s work, see for instance Hans Peter Schwarz, *Der konservative Anarchist: Politik und Zeitkritik Ernst Jüngers* (Freiburg i.B., 1962); J. P. Stern, *Ernst Jünger, a Writer of our Time* (Cambridge, 1953); Helmut Kaiser, *Mythos, Rausch und Reaktion. Der Weg Gottfried Benns und Ernst Jüngers* (Berlin, 1962).

4. For a detailed account of E.J.'s activities and writings during the Weimar years, see H. M. Ridley, *National Socialism and Literature. Five Writers in Search of an Ideology*, Ph.D. Diss. University of Cambridge (1967).

5. So laconic was it that attempts were made to enlist it in the cause of the right-wing heroicization of war. But its nationalist champions were discomfited to learn that Renn, whose real name was Arnold Vieth von Golssenau, had joined the Communist Party a year before. After Renn's arrest in 1933, the Nazis spent several months trying in vain to persuade him to join their ranks, on the strength of the impact made by his war book.

6. A bookseller's statistic indicates the special appeal of Carossa's book. In the first five years after publication, which coincided with the stabilization of the Weimar Republic, the book sold only in moderate numbers. Between 1929 and 1934 the rate at which it sold increased substantially. But from 1934 to 1938 sales accelerated even faster. (Figures in Donald Ray Richards, *The German Bestseller in the 20th Century. A complete Bibliography and Analysis 1915–1940* (Berne, 1968).) In other words it joined with the literature of the '*innere Emigration*' (see pp. 62–9) in offering consolation and vague hope to those who saw themselves at the mercy of forces beyond their control, which they had in fact themselves helped to unleash.

7. See J. P. Stern, *On Realism* (London/Boston, 1973), p. 50 and Stern, *Ernst Jünger, op. cit.*, pp. 31–3.

8. Under the title 'Der grosse Krieg der Weissen Männer' the cycle includes *Die Zeit ist reif* (1957); *Junge Frau von 1914* (1931); *Erziehung vor Verdun* (1935); *Grischa; Die Feuerpause* (1954); *Einsetzung eines Königs* (1937).

Chapter Two

1. For the following I have drawn on John Willett, *Expressionism* (London, 1970); Eberhard Lämmert, 'Das expressionistische Verkündigungsdrama' in *Der deutsche Expressionismus. Formen und Gestalten*, Hans Steffen (ed.) (Göttingen, 1965); Kasimir Edschmid, *Über den Expressionismus in der Literatur und die neue Dichtung* (Berlin, 1920); Walter H. Sokel, *The Writer in Extremis. Expressionism in 20th Century German Literature* (Stanford, 1959); Paul Raabe, 'Das literarische Leben im Expressionismus. Eine historische Skizze' in *Die Zeitschriften und Sammlungen des literarischen Expressionismus* (Stuttgart, 1964); Eva Kolinsky, *Engagierter Expressionismus. Politik und Literatur zwischen Weltkrieg und Weimarer Republik* (Stuttgart, 1970); Jürgen Rühle, *Literatur und Revolution* (Köln/Berlin, 1960); Günther Rühle, *Theater für die Republik 1917–33 im Spiegel der Kritik* (Frankfurt, 1967); Roy Pascal, *From Naturalism to Expressionism, op. cit.*; Friedrich Albrecht, *Deutsche Schriftsteller in der Entscheidung, op. cit.*; Peter Gay, *Weimar Culture. The Outsider as Insider* (London, 1969); Gordon A. Craig, 'Engagement and Neutrality in Weimar Germany', *Journal of Contemporary History*, vol. II, no. 2 (April 1967).

2. Walter Benjamin, 'Karl Kraus', *Illuminationen*, Siegfried Unseld (ed.) (Frankfurt a.M., 1961), p. 404.

3. Walter H. Sokel, 'Brecht und der Expressionismus', in *Die sogenannten Zwanziger Jahre*, Reinhold Grimm and Jost Hermand (eds.) (Bad Homburg/Berlin/Zürich, 1970), p. 48.

4. Peter Szondi, *Theorie des modernen Dramas* (edition suhrkamp 27, Frankfurt, 1966), p. 108.

5. Pascal, *From Naturalism to Expressionism*, p. 196.

6. See Lämmert, *op. cit.*; Keller, *Nationalismus und Literatur, op. cit.*, p. 138 ff. (cp. his analysis of the 'fatal mixture of pietism and patriotism' in Walter Flex's best-selling war book *Der Wanderer zwischen beiden Welten*, p. 48 ff.); and J. P. Stern, *Hitler: the Führer and the People* (London, 1975) esp. 'The Language of Sacrifice', 'The Religious

Expectation and its Ritual' and 'A Society longing for Transcendence'. For a case study of Messianism in the novels of Alfred Döblin, who showed early affinities with Expressionism, see W. G. Sebald, 'Zum Thema Messianismus im Werk Döblins', *Neophilologus*, vol. LIX, no. 3 (1975), pp. 421–34. Some of these links were anticipated in the attack on the Expressionists, above all Johst and Arnolt Bronnen, launched for dubious reasons and with characteristic crudeness by the Muscovite champions of 'socialist realism' in the mid-thirties (cf. n. 14 below).

7. See Wolfgang Rothe (ed.), *Der Aktivismus 1915–1920*, DTV 625 (München, 1969), esp. the introduction and Hiller's policy statements; also Friedrich Albrecht, *op. cit.*, pp. 66–9, pp. 84–6 and pp. 497–501 for the 1918 programme of the 'Rat geistiger Arbeiter'.

8. For biographical details, see John M. Spalek, 'Ernst Toller: the need for a new estimate', *The German Quarterly*, vol. XXXIX, no. 4 (November, 1966) and 'Ernst Tollers Vortragstätigkeit und seine Hilfsaktionen im Exil', *Exil und Innere Emigration II*, Peter Uwe Hohendahl and Egon Schwarz (eds.) (Frankfurt, 1973). I am indebted to Dr Dorothea Klein for allowing me to read her searching, informative and stimulating thesis *Der Wandel der dramatischen Darstellungsform im Werk Ernst Tollers (1919–1930)*, Diss. Bochum (1968). See also Walter H. Sokel, 'Ernst Toller' in *Deutsche Literatur im 20. Jahrhundert. Strukturen und Gestalten*, Otto Mann and Wolfgang Rothe (eds.), 5th Edn. (Bern/München, 1967).

9. Pascal, *From Naturalism to Expressionism*, p. 122.

10. Bertolt Brecht, *Gesammelte Werke 19, Schriften zur Literatur und Kunst 2*, werkausgabe (edition suhrkamp, Frankfurt, 1967), p. 304.

11. For accounts of party policy, critical debates, literary developments and the contribution of individual writers, see e.g., Albrecht, *Deutsche Schriftsteller in der Entscheidung, op. cit.*; *Zur Tradition der sozialistischen Literatur in Deutschland. Eine Auswahl von Dokumenten*, ed. with commentary by the Deutsche Akademie der Künste zu Berlin, Sektion Dichtkunst und Sprachpflege, Abteilung Geschichte der sozialistischen Literatur, 2nd Edn. (Berlin/Weimar, 1967); Alfred Klein, *Im Auftrag ihrer Klasse. Weg und Leistung der deutschen Arbeiterschriftsteller 1918–1933* (Berlin/Weimar, 1972); Walter Fähnders and Martin Rector, *Linksradikalismus und Literatur. Untersuchungen zur Geschichte der sozialistischen Literatur in der Weimarer Republik*, 2 vols. (Reinbek bei Hamburg, 1974); Wolfgang Rothe (ed.), *Die deutsche Literatur in der Weimarer Republik* (Stuttgart, 1974); and above all

Helga Gallas, *Marxistische Literaturtheorie. Kontroversen im Bund proletarisch-revolutionärer Schriftsteller* (Sammlung Luchterhand 19, Neuwied/Berlin, 1971).

12. See J. P. Stern, *On Realism*, p. 53 and § 99.

13. Gallas, *op. cit.*, p. 88.

14. The two debates were separate but revolved around the same issues. Lukács' critique of Expressionism ('Grösse und Verfall des E.') appeared in 1934. He found it 'too imprecise in its idea of "bourgeois" and "revolution", too clamorous in its language, too egocentric in its attitude and altogether too incapable of conveying any but a fragmentary view of the world to live up to its progressive pretensions and admitted achievements in stimulating opposition to the First World War' (Willett, p. 217). The attack was renewed by Kurella in 1937 when he claimed that it was inevitable that a whole-hearted Expressionist should end up on the side of the Nazis. A series of articles for and against Expressionism and the Lukács aesthetic then appeared in the emigré periodical *Das Wort* in Moscow. See Hans Jürgen Schmitt, *Die Expressionismus-Debatte. Zur marxistischen Theorie des Realismus* (Frankfurt, 1973); David R. Bathrick, 'Moderne Kunst und Klassenkampf. Die Expressionismus-Debatte in der Exilzeitschrift *Das Wort*', in *Exil und Innere Emigration*, Reinhold Grimm and Jost Hermand (eds.) (Frankfurt, 1972); Franz Schonauer, 'Expressionismus und Faschismus. Eine Diskussion aus dem Jahre 1938', *Literatur und Kritik*, Band 1, Nr. 7 (1966), pp. 44–54.

For the Lukács-Seghers exchange, see Georg Lukács, *Probleme des Realismus* (Berlin, 1955).

See also Brecht's notes 'Über den Realismus', 'Volkstümlichkeit und Realismus', 'Notizen über realistische Schreibweise' in *Gesammelte Werke 19* (cf. Note 11); and Klaus Völker, 'Brecht und Lukács: Analyse einer Meinungsverschiedenheit', *Kursbuch 7* (1966), pp. 80–101.

15. Spalek, 'Ernst Toller: the need for a new estimate', *loc. cit.*, pp. 594–5.

16. See his somewhat over-generous tribute to it in *Gesammelte Werke 19*, *op. cit.*, p. 330.

17. See C. D. Innes, *Erwin Piscator's Political Theatre* (Cambridge, 1972); Helga Gallas, *op. cit.*, pp. 94–5.

18. For statistics, see Gallas, p. 94; for limitations, see David Caute, *The Illusion. An Essay on Politics, Theatre and the Novel* (London, 1971), p. 68.

19. See Inge Diersen, *Seghers-Studien. Interpretationen von Werken*

aus den Jahren 1926–1935. Ein Beitrag zu Entwicklungsproblemen der modernen deutschen Epik (Berlin, 1965), introduction.

20. Ernst Fischer, *An Opposing Man*, transl. Peter and Betty Ross, with an introduction by John Berger (London, 1974), p. 5.

21. Though even here only by virtue of a solipsistic defence mechanism. See W. A. J. Steer, *'Baal*: A Key to Brecht's Communism', *German Life and Letters*, vol. XIX (1965), pp. 40–51.

22. Most of them between 1932 (65,000) and 1935 (315,000). Even more worryingly, it was still selling a decade ago: by 1965 sales had reached 780,000 (Richards, *The German Bestseller*, p. 4 and Keller, *Nationalismus und Literatur*, p. 260, n. 22).

23. See A. J. Nicholls, *Weimar and the Rise of Hitler* (London, 1968), pp. 94–6.

24. See Ridley, *National Socialism and Literature, op. cit.*, p. 104, 109 n, 115 ff. There too can be found details of Grimm's career, his publicistic writing and his relationship with the Nazis. After 1933 he protested his 'independence' of the regime he had helped to win power. He even instituted an annual *Dichtertreffen* at Lippoldsberg from 1936 onwards, designed to rival the official Nazi literary gatherings at Weimar. It was attended by such writers as Carossa, Dwinger, Kolbenheyer, Von Salomon and R. A. Schröder. On Grimm, see also Keller, *Nationalismus und Literatur, op. cit.*, pp. 122–33 and Francis L. Carsten, '*Volk ohne Raum*. A Note on Hans Grimm', *Journal of Contemporary History*, vol. II, no. 2 (April, 1967), pp. 221–7.

25. Ridley, *op cit.*, p. 105.

26. This was an attempt to combine anti-capitalism and anti-Western feeling with a militant German nationalism in emulation of and in alliance with Soviet Russia. Cf. Kurt Sontheimer, *Antidemokratisches Denken, op. cit.*, and Otto Ernst Schüddekopf, *Linke Leute von rechts. Die national-revolutionären Minderheiten und der Kommunismus in der Weimarer Republik* (Stuttgart, 1960). Jünger was for a time associated with these circles. They were 'neutralized' along with the left wing of the NSDAP in deference to industry and the bourgeoisie.

27. See R. G. L. Waite, *Vanguard of Nazism. The Free Corps Movement in Postwar Germany 1918–1923* (Cambridge Mass., 1952).

Chapter Three

1. I have borrowed this rendering from Helmut Gruber, '*Neue Sachlichkeit* and the World War', *GLL*, vol. XX, no. 2 (January 1967). For the concept itself, see Helmut Lethen, *Neue Sachlichkeit*

1924–1932. Studien zur Literatur des 'Weissen Sozialismus' (Stuttgart, 1970); Horst Denkler, 'Sache und Stil. Die Theorie der "Neuen Sachlichkeit" und ihre Auswirkungen auf Kunst und Dichtung', *Wirkendes Wort*, Jhg. 18, Heft 3 (1968), pp. 167–85; and Wolfgang Rothe (ed.), *Die deutsche Literatur in der Weimarer Republik, op. cit.*

2. Lukács, 'Reportage oder Gestaltung?', a review article concerned with Ottwalt's novel *Denn sie wissen, was sie tun.* Now in *Zur Tradition der sozialistischen Literatur in Deutschland, op. cit.*, together with Ottwalt's rejoinder.

3. *Des Kaisers Kulis. Roman der deutschen Kriegsflotte* (Berlin, 1930). See p. 32.

4. For a list of the changes and a general discussion of their significance, see Dorothea Klein, *op. cit.*, p. 153 ff and pp. 236–7.

5. Jost Hermand, *Unbequeme Literatur. Eine Beispielreihe* (Heidelberg, 1971), p. 163.

6. See J. P. Stern *On Realism, op. cit.*, p. 122 and p. 143.

7. Piscator's new Theater am Nollendorfplatz opened with the premiere of Toller's play. But Piscator found much to criticize in Toller's text: it was too subjective, too emotional and the issues too confused. He thus adapted the text for production, even to the extent of writing in new scenes without Toller's consent. At the end of his version, after a new affirmative last line, the audience spontaneously burst into the Internationale. See Innes, *op. cit.*, p. 128, Klein, p. 118 ff. and Hermand, *Unbequeme Literatur, op. cit.*, pp. 128–49.

8. Both Fritz von Unruh (in *Phaea*, 1930) and Kaiser (in *Nebeneinander*, 1923) likewise depicted the catastrophe of the Expressionist character in a clash with objective reality: cf. Grimm/Hermand, 'Zwischen Expressionismus und Faschismus. Bemerkungen zum Drama der Zwanziger Jahre' in *Die sogenannten Zwanziger Jahre, op. cit.*

9. It seems likely that Reger borrowed his classification from the sociologist Werner Sombart who in *Der Bourgeois* (1913) had distinguished between the heroic adventurer, the patriarch and the calculating dealer, the *Händler*. For details, see Pascal, *From Naturalism to Expressionism*, p. 31.

10. See Walter Bussmann, 'Politische Ideologien zwischen Monarchie und Weimarer Republik. Ein Beitrag zur Ideengeschichte der Weimarer Republik', *Historische Zeitschrift*, Bd. 190, Heft 1 (February 1960), pp. 55–77; for the caveat, see Peter Gay, *Weimar Culture* (London, 1969), pp. 24–5.

11. For an appraisal of Mann's political ideas and attitudes, see Kurt

BIRKBECK LIBRARY COLLEGE

Sontheimer, *Thomas Mann und die Deutschen* (Fischer-Bücherei 650, Frankfurt/Hamburg, 1965); Erich Heller, *The Ironic German. A Study of Thomas Mann* (London, 1958), esp. 'The Conservative Imagination'; T. J. Reed, *Thomas Mann. The Uses of Tradition* (Oxford, 1974), esp. 'Unpolitics: War thoughts 1914–1918' and 'Republic: Politics 1919–1933'; Ernst Keller, *Der Unpolitische Deutsche. Eine Studie zu den 'Betrachtungen eines Unpolitischen' von Thomas Mann* (Bern/München, 1965); J. P. Stern, *Hitler, op. cit.*, pp. 30–3; Günter Hartung, 'Bertolt Brecht und Thomas Mann. Über Alternativen in Kunst und Politik', *Weimarer Beiträge* 12 (1966).

12. J. P. Stern talks of the 'whole complex relationship between the demagogue and the masses' and of 'the predicament of the European liberal mind in the grip of the demagogue's will'. See his *Thomas Mann* (New York/London, 1967), p. 25.

13. For an even more pessimistic interpretation of Mann's story, see J. P. Stern, *Hitler, op. cit.*, pp. 67–8.

14. Another decade was to elapse before Mann devoted an essay to 'Bruder Hitler'.

15. 'Von deutscher Republik' (Foreword to printed version), *Gesammelte Werke in zwölf Bänden*, Band XI, *Reden und Aufsätze 3*, (Frankfurt, 1960), p. 809.

Chapter Four

1. I have drawn on the following: Ernst Loewy, *Literatur unterm Hakenkreuz, op. cit.*; J. P. Stern, *Hitler : the Führer and the People, op. cit.*; Rolf Geissler, *Dekadenz und Heroismus, op. cit.*; Albrecht Schöne, *Über politische Lyrik im 20. Jahrhundert* (Kleine Vandenhoeck-Reihe 228–9, Göttingen, 1965); Joseph Wulf, *Literatur und Dichtung im Dritten Reich. Eine Dokumentation* (rororo Taschenbuch-Ausgabe, Reinbek bei Hamburg, 1966); Dietrich Strothmann, *Nationalsozialistische Literaturpolitik. Ein Beitrag zur Publizistik im Dritten Reich*, 2nd Edn. (Bonn, 1963); Ernst Keller, *Nationalismus und Literatur, op. cit.*, 'Das letzte Reich'.

The Germanist will find a grotesque sidelight on Nazi literary policy in H. G. Atkins, *German Literature through Nazi Eyes* (London, 1941).

2. 'Der Kunstbericht soll weniger Wertung, als vielmehr Darstellung und damit Würdigung sein', quoted by Geissler, p. 30.

3. Quoted in Walter A. Berendsohn, *Die humanistische Front. Einführung in die deutsche Emigranten-Literatur*, Erster Teil (Zürich, 1946), p. 25.

4. Franz Schonauer, *Deutsche Literatur im Dritten Reich. Versuch einer Darstellung in polemisch-didaktischer Absicht* (Olten/Freiburg, 1961), p. 86.

5. For the following see esp. Schöne, *Über politische Lyrik*.

6. *Ibid.*, p. 20.

7. See Willett, *Expressionism, op. cit.*, p. 198 ff.

8. For accounts of Benn's relationship with National Socialism, see e.g., Walter Lennig, *Gottfried Benn*, Rowohlts-Monographien (Reinbek bei Hamburg, 1962); Helmut Kaiser, *Mythos, Rausch und Reaktion, op. cit.*; Ridley, *National Socialism and Literature, op. cit.*; Peter de Mendelssohn, *Der Geist in der Despotie. Versuche über die moralischen Möglichkeiten des Intellektuellen in der totalitären Gesellschaft* (Berlin-Grunewald, 1953).

9. These included 'Der neue Staat und die Intellektuellen' (April 1933); 'Antwort an die literarischen Emigranten' (May 1933); 'Zucht und Zukunft' (October 1933); 'Expressionismus' (November 1933); 'Rede auf Marinetti' (March 1934); 'Rede auf Stefan George' (April 1934).

10. Many of the most significant works are discussed in Wolfgang Brekle, 'Die antifaschistische Literatur in Deutschland (1933–1945)', *Weimarer Beiträge*, vol. XVI, Heft 6 (1970), pp. 67 ff.

11. My account is based on the following: Reinhold Grimm, 'Innere Emigration als Lebensform' in Grimm/Hermand (eds.), *Exil und Innere Emigration, op. cit.*; Gunter Groll, *De Profundis. Deutsche Lyrik in dieser Zeit. Eine Anthologie aus zwölf Jahren* (München, 1946); W. A. Berendsohn, *Die humanistische Front, op. cit.*; F. Schonauer, *Deutsche Literatur im Dritten Reich, op. cit.*; Charles W. Hoffman, *Opposition Poetry in Nazi Germany* (Berkeley and Los Angeles, 1962); Hoffman, 'Opposition und Innere Emigration. Zwei Aspekte des "anderen Deutschlands" ', in *Exil und Innere Emigration II*, Peter Uwe Hohendahl and Egon Schwarz (eds.) (Frankfurt, 1973); H. R. Klieneberger, *The Christian Writers of the Inner Emigration* (The Hague/Paris, 1968); Heinz D. Osterle, 'The Other Germany. Resistance to the Third Reich in German Literature', *The Germany Quarterly*, vol. 41 (1968), p. 1 ff.; Keller, *Nationalismus und Literatur, op. cit.*, 'Das letzte Reich'.

12. For documents and commentary, see J. F. G. Grosser, *Die grosse Kontroverse. Ein Briefwechsel um Deutschland* (Hamburg etc., 1963).

13. The term '*Sklavensprache*' which occurs repeatedly in discussions of the '*innere Emigration*' seems to have been coined by the novelist

Hans Werner Richter in 'Die Gruppe 47', *Moderna Sprak* 58 (1964); cited by Karl Otto Conrady, 'Deutsche Literaturwissenschaft und Drittes Reich' in *Germanistik—eine deutsche Wissenschaft*, 2nd Edn. (edition suhrkamp 204, Frankfurt, 1967), p. 78.

14. Osterle, *loc. cit.*, pp. 5–6, echoing Schonauer, p. 126.

15. R. Grimm, *loc. cit.*, p. 72, and Keller, *Nationalismus und Literatur*, on Jochen Klepper.

16. Theodor Zielkowski, 'Form als Protest' in Grimm/Hermand, *Exil und Innere Emigration, op. cit.*

17. For his relations with the regime, see Sumner Kirschner, 'Some Documents relating to Ernst Wiechert's "Inward Emigration" ', *The German Quarterly*, vol. 38 (1965). In his story 'Der weisse Büffel' (read in public in 1937) we are presented with a Schillerian martyrdom, again involving a penitent ruler to ensure the eventual reconciliation with the spiritual principle.

18. Strothmann, *op. cit.*, p. 379. Keller notes that it received a 'positive' evaluation from the Amt Rosenberg and that it fulfilled two major criteria of Nazi fiction, 'Idyllik und Heroismus', *op. cit.*, p. 182.

19. Richards, *The German Bestseller, op. cit.*, gives a figure of 23,000; but Strothmann, p. 378, n. 50 cites a much lower figure of 12,000 in the first year of publication.

Chapter Five

1. See Hans-Albert Walter, *Bedrohung und Verfolgung bis 1933*, vol. I of his *Deutsche Exilliteratur 1933–1950* (Sammlung Luchterhand, Neuwied/Berlin, 1972). This work, comprising in all nine volumes of which three have appeared to date, promises to become a standard work of reference on German exile literature.

2. For the following account I am indebted to: Jost Hermand, 'Schreiben in der Fremde' in Grimm/Hermand (eds.), *Exil und Innere Emigration, op. cit.*; W. A. Berendsohn, *Die humanistische Front, op. cit.*; Egon Schwarz and Matthias Wegner (eds.), *Verbannung. Aufzeichnungen Deutscher Schriftsteller im Exil* (Hamburg, 1964); Matthias Wegner, *Exil und Literatur. Deutsche Schriftsteller im Ausland 1933–1945* (Frankfurt/Bonn, 1967); Hans-Albert Walter, 'Das Bild Deutschlands im Exilroman', *Neue Rundschau* 1966, pp. 437–58 and 'Deutsche Literatur im Exil', *Merkur* 273 (1971), pp. 71–7; Manfred Durzak (ed.), *Die Deutsche Exilliteratur 1933–1945* (Stuttgart, 1973); Peter Uwe Hohendahl and Egon Schwarz (eds.), *Exil und Innere Emigration II* (Frankfurt, 1973);

and the anthology of documents, memoirs and essays in Heinz Ludwig Arnold (ed.), *Deutsche Literatur im Exil 1933–1945. Dokumente und Materialien*, 2 vols. (Frankfurt a.M., 1974).

3. On the changing image of Germany in the prose fiction of these years, see Walter's article 'Das Bild Deutschlands . . .'

4. See Frank Trommler, 'Emigration und Nachkriegsliteratur' in Grimm/Hermand, *Exil und Innere Emigration*.

5. In conversation with Friedrich Wolf; cited in Hans Mayer, *Bertolt Brecht und die Tradition* (sonderreihe DTV, München, 1965), p. 8. Other useful works from the vast bibliography on Brecht: Reinhold Grimm, *Bertolt Brecht : die Struktur seines Werkes*, 3rd edn. (Nürnberg, 1962); Volker Klotz, *Bertolt Brecht. Versuch über das Werk* (Darmstadt, 1957); *Theaterarbeit. Sechs Aufführungen des Berliner Ensembles* (Dresden, n.d.); Martin Esslin, *Brecht : A Choice of Evils* (London, 1959) and *Bertolt Brecht* (New York, 1969); Walter Hinck, *Die Dramaturgie des späten Brecht*, 3rd edn. (Göttingen, 1962).

6. J. P. Stern has pointed out that, however much we (or the author) suggest rational explanations for Leverkühn's illness, a final doubt remains. See *Thomas Mann, op. cit.*, p. 39.

7. See J. P. Stern, 'History and Allegory in Thomas Mann's *Doktor Faustus*. An inaugural lecture delivered at University College, London on 1 March 1973'.

8. Thomas Mann, *Doktor Faustus. Das Leben des deutschen Tonsetzers Adrian Leverkühn, erzählt von einem Freunde* (Frankfurt a.M., 1960), p. 535.

9. The debate on just this aspect of Mann's novel continues. E. M. Butler in *The Fortunes of Faust* (Cambridge, 1952) was an early critic of the symbolic validity of the composer-hero. Ronald Gray's *The German Tradition in Literature 1871–1945* (Cambridge, 1965) condemned the implications of the ending as 'absurd or horrible'. J. P. Stern takes issue with these arguments in the Inaugural Lecture mentioned above, suggesting 'that on the level of specific events and individual ideas the allegorical parallels are incomplete and intermittent, implying and leaving room for the freedom of the individual from a total determinism'. See also Erich Heller, *The Ironic German, op. cit.*, chapter VIII and 'Faust's Damnation' in *The Artist's Journey into the Interior and other Essays* (London, 1966); Roy Pascal, *The German Novel* (Manchester, 1956), esp. Chapter IX; T. J. Reed, *Thomas Mann, op. cit.*, 'Reckoning'; Erich Kahler, *The Orbit of Thomas Mann* (Princeton, 1969); Gunilla Bergsten, *Thomas Manns 'Doktor Faustus'* :

Untersuchungen zu den Quellen und zur Struktur des Romans (Stockholm, 1963).

Conclusion

1. See Peter Schneider, 'Politische Dichtung. Ihre Grenzen und Möglichkeiten' in Peter Stein (ed.), *Theorie der politischen Dichtung* (München, 1973).

2. Octavia Paz argues that modern (post-symbolist) poetry moves between two poles, the 'magical' and the 'revolutionary'. Both attempt to reconcile the alienated consciousness with the world outside. The 'magical' consists in a desire to return to nature by dissolving the self-consciousness that separates us from it, to lose ourselves in animal innocence and liberate ourselves from history. The 'revolutionary' aspiration demands that the distance between man and nature, word and thing, be abolished through a conquest of the historical world. Quoted in Michael Hamburger, *The Truth of Poetry* (Harmondsworth, 1972), p. 44.

3. Hans Magnus Enzensberger, 'Poesie und Politik' in *Einzelheiten II*, (edition suhrkamp 87, Frankfurt, n.d.). On this point he echoes a Platonic argument, though he stands Plato's political conclusion on its head: 'For the introduction of a new kind of music must be shunned as imperilling the whole state, since styles of music are never disturbed without affecting the most important political institutions.' (*The Republic*, Book IV, §424, translated by Davies and Vaughan.)